Voices From Beyond

Table of Contents

Preface..vi

Ch 1: Escape from Reality..............................3

Ch 2: Odd Actions.....................................11

Ch 3: Others Notice Change............................18

Ch 4: Sick Mind.......................................25

Ch 5: Inside the Asylum...............................31

Ch 6: The Escape......................................38

Ch 7: Lost in Dallas..................................43

Ch 8: Rock Bottom.....................................46

Ch 9: Needle in a Haystack............................53

Ch 10: Locked Ward....................................58

Ch 11: Released.......................................67

Ch 12: God's Voice....................................72

Ch 13: Settling Down..................................87

Ch 14: Our First House................................90

Ch 15: Another Move..................................92

Ch 16: Pregnant Again..............................103

Ch 17: Leaving Our Church Family..............108

Ch 18: God Reveals Himself.......................114

Ch 19: The Tupperware Story.....................139

Ch 20: Knowing Fear.................................143

Ch 21: Garage Sale...................................153

Ch 22: Cleaning Floors..............................160

Ch 23: Home Again...................................169

Ch 24: Car Wreck......................................176

Ch 25: Practice Faith.................................184

Ch 26: God Meets My Needs.....................191

Ch 27: Secrets Revealed...........................197

Ch 28: Why Weddings?..............................201

Ch 29: God Yells!......................................219

Ch 30: Knowing Myself..............................224

Ch 31: The New House..............................229

Ch 32: Closing the Shop............................236

Voices From Beyond

By: Ann Norris

Copyright 2016

This book is dedicated to my husband, Jeff, who loves me with an exceptional love. God provided him as my rock and fortress through these storms of life.

I love you, honey, as much as I know how.

Ch 33: Changes Come..............................246

Ch 34: The Bible Study............................248

Ch 35: Manic / Depressive........................261

Ch 36: Autoharp Champion......................264

Ch 37: Insane Again?...............................266

Ch 38: Course Correction.........................268

Ch 39: Ovarian Cancer.............................270

Ch 40: Total Peace...................................273

To My Readers.......................................274

Acknowledgements.................................276

About the Author....................................278

Preface

At age twenty I had a mental breakdown and was institutionalized for six months. I experienced fourteen shock treatments and the dreadful padded cell. The diagnosis wasn't pretty. I was labeled a severe paranoid schizophrenic and released into my husband's care.

This is the story of my journey from insanity to sanity. I am able to control my fears and function not only in a normal fashion, but go beyond that and excel. All of this without continued medication or professional personal counseling.

Many who know me will be shocked to hear I was ever mentally imbalanced, for today, I am stable and have a clear mind. I live abundantly, enjoying the benefits of good relationships and peace.

This is not a "how to" book. It is simply my story, dealing with my condition in a way that worked for me.

All scriptures in this book are my paraphrases from the King James Bible.

....

Romans 12:2
Don't be like everyone else in this world, but be changed by the renewing of your mind, so you can prove what is good and acceptable and what God expects of all of us.

Revelation 12: 11
And they overcame the evil one by the blood of the Lamb and their testimonies; and they were devoted to truth even if it meant they would be killed.

Ephesians 6:12
For we don't struggle against what we can see with our physical eyes, but rather, the spiritual principals and powers that are the rulers of evil in this world. We fight against spiritual wickedness in high places.

PART I

THE VISION

Chapter 1: Escape from Reality

The old house was so empty it echoed. Its original hardwood floors had lost their luster years ago. This wasn't a home, but a place people only rented and left as soon as they could afford to go elsewhere or got evicted. I was no exception.

I paid a month's rent up front and moved in. For fifty dollars I purchased and old gas stove and small refrigerator, then, spent the day with bleach water and rags removing the grime and rat castings from both. Admiring my work, I knew my dated, thrifty purchases were spotlessly clean. I was determined to make the best of a bad situation. By restoring them, they had a new start in life. I longed for that too.

The house smelled strongly antiseptic, but this scent would soon dissipate and return to the musty odor that things and old people emit when waiting for death. It wasn't the optimum location, but it was a place where I had no restrictions. Or so I thought.
I sniffed my raw, wrinkled hands that cried for moisture, but I had no lotion.

Exhausted, I eased down on a bare mattress on the floor. It had been days since I slept. Eyes wide open, I waited for the night. I was barely twenty years old and spending my first night alone.

The vocal music scholarships you were offered the last year of high school are of no use now. College is no option. You are a wife and mother living on your husband's military salary. He doesn't make much as a private. You have no job and barely three-hundred dollars in savings. The five dollars in my purse is not enough for necessities. Minimum wage won't pay for babysitting and gas to get to work. Your mother thinks you don't know what to do with a new baby, and you don't. Now what will you do?"

Depressed, I resigned myself to diapers and bottles and low income for the rest of my life. I felt so guilty and worthless for getting pregnant before I married. In the 1960's that was a terrible thing to do. I faced a future with little hope and nobody to talk with about my problems. I only wished for some solution.

Listening to the distant rumblings of a coming storm, I

watched as the sky changed. The storm was coming fast. Huge domes of grey clouds grew like bacteria in a Petri dish. The first incoming raindrops struck the thin windows like rounds of artillery.

This was tornado country and I was familiar with winds that blew over large trees as easily as snapping a stick of celery. I lifted myself from the mattress and went to the front window, searching for a funnel cloud. To the west, the sun was going down fast, getting out of storm's way. To the east, an enormous wall of churning darkness looked the way I felt, boiling with anger and ready to blame anybody but myself. Soon it began its tantrum.

Small hailstones popped hard against the windowpanes. I stepped back hoping the gusting wind wouldn't crack the windows and send shards inward. I watched from the center of the room as the storm raged. Waves of hard rain swirled in a furious dance. Lightning bolts hit the ground and thunder rattled the bones of the old house.

I was powerless and afraid. The weather outside was very threatening. Hoping the storm would soon finish,

I curled up the mattress and drew my arms around my shoulders.

My teeth chattered. My eyes darted from window to window. Like a caged animal, my heart was beating as fast as hummingbird wings. I expected the roof to rip apart any moment. Trying to keep calm, I thought. *Nothing is going to happen to you. Breathe deeply. You can handle this.*

Suddenly, the front door blew open and slammed hard against the inner wall. I instinctively drew into a fetal position and shut my eyes, hands over my head. Nothing else happened.

You're okay. The door latch failed. Go close it before the rain soaks the floor.

As I sat up, I saw in the doorway an abnormally tall man, the most beautiful man I'd ever seen. His skin was smooth and hairless like a baby's, but his body rippled with muscles. He was flawless with wavy blonde hair and light blue eyes, as transparent as water.

He was barefoot, wearing a white karate suit with a

rope tied at his waist. The rope looked new, sculpted, perfect, without fraying.

I blinked my eyes and struggled with what I saw. With a rich-as-velvet tone, his thoughts penetrated my mind inaudibly, though clearly with authority.

"Don't be afraid. I am here to help you. You are at a crossroad in your life. I can lead you to freedom from the mess you made of your choices and all the responsibilities you have."

I liked what I heard.

He continued, "There will be no limitations for you. You can be the incarnation of Jesus Christ if you wish. You will be the 'second coming'. Really, anyone could be. It is only a matter of total submission to my instructions. No one else has been dedicated enough."

What kind of man is this? This is not normal.

He explained, "I will give you moment- by- moment instructions in your mind. You must be completely obedient to my voice, without hesitation, if you are to have this new life I promise."

I entertained that thought. To have the power of God was overwhelming.
Suddenly I grasped, *I can do anything and have anything I want if I obey his voice.* I really wanted to believe his promise.

I dropped my eyes, totally concentrating on the concept. The idea of such strong empowerment was something I never considered. I savored the possibilities.

This man's presence was so convincing. I believed everything he said as absolute truth. My thoughts skipped around the idea.

That's incredible! YOU are chosen to be the "Second Coming of Christ"! Was it possible that I was the only human being who had received the invitation to obey the "voice"? Surely many others must have had the same invitation, yet somehow they failed to be totally committed to the required obedience. That's why the world waited for the second manifestation of Christ. If only I could be the ONE! It was so astounding and yet so simple it made sense. If Jesus Christ came once in the flesh, He could do it again. He only needed a body to fulfill the mission.

The promise of having the power of Christ shook my soul, like suddenly being privy to the perimeters of the vast universe.

I officially stepped out of reality into another world, a four- dimensional world where the "voice" had the ability to accomplish anything, using my body. When I looked up again the messenger had vanished.

Rain water stood in a puddle at the open door. I closed the door and mopped the water from the floor, knowing I had seen a messenger from God or some kind of unearthly being. I had no idea how much time had passed, but the storm had quelled and the air smelled fresh and clean.
My concern for the future left with the storm. I felt rejuvenated…reborn.

Excited, I didn't sleep for the remainder of the night. My mind chewed on the thoughts I'd heard. All my forebodings were swept away. I didn't have a care.

The angel sold me with the word "freedom". I would not be accountable for my choices because I would not be making them! I would be following orders from the "voice", totally free. I determined that night to get on with my new life.

Chapter 2: Odd Actions

The next morning was bright and clear. The air bristled with energy and so did I, even though I hadn't slept much. I began listening intently for instructions from the "voice." While getting dressed, I missed a pair of shoes I wanted. I realized they were at my mom's house, half a mile away. I had no car or phone. Reason told me to wear whatever I had. Mom would drop by in the afternoon and I could go for another load of my things, including all my shoes. But then I heard the "voice" in my head.

"Why do you need a car? Look outside the window. There is your answer."

A boy rested in the middle of the street astride his bicycle. He was enjoying his summer vacation, totally unaware I was watching him.

I stepped outside and strode over where he stood. "Hi", I said. "I'm new to the neighborhood... moved in a couple of days ago. Do you live nearby?"
Avoiding eye contact with me, he ducked his head.

"Yeah," he agreed, but offered no other comment as he sipped from the nickel Coke in his hand.

"Nice bike you have," I ventured. "Could I borrow it for about an hour?" Explaining further, "I forgot to get some of the things for the house. They are a few blocks away and I don't have a car. Maybe you'd loan me your bike for awhile?"

I saw the distrust in his eyes and added, "I'll give you five dollars if you will."

His eyes brightened. Five dollars was more than he could earn mowing lawns all day.

I pressed the money into his hand and he eagerly dismounted the bike, thrusting it towards me. I hopped astride and pushed off.

The "voice" was right. I could do anything I wanted if I just listened and obeyed. Somehow I trusted I wouldn't need the money.

Days later after I finished moving, other instructions came from the "voice" that gave me more confidence in his instructions. I was concerned about all the weight I'd gained while pregnant. Still overweight by fifty pounds, I turned side to side, looking in a mirror. Then I heard the "voice" say, "If you want to lose weight fast, stop eating. When you are really hungry then drink a glass of milk and take a vitamin pill."

So I did just that. My energy level never waned as the weight began to drop. The "voice" was right again. I did things that seemed perfectly normal to me though disconcerting to those around me. But by that time, my trust in the "voice" had grown.

As I was lowering my sleeping baby onto his stomach in the crib the "voice" suggested, "If you want him to sleep longer so you can get more work done, cover his head with a pillow to block out the noise." So, I obeyed, and it worked.

I longed to have a good friend who would understand my predicament and could share some time with me, but all my friends were at college, working towards their goals.

One morning I dressed my baby, loaded him in the stroller and walked to my former high school. I thought I'd casually drop in to see my choir director and voice coach. The fact that he would be busy teaching didn't matter to me. I needed a friend.

He was surprised to see me but never acted inconvenienced. So while his class waited for instruction, he sat and chatted with me for a long time. Years later, he laughed when he told me he hadn't known what to do. He was always glad to see his former students, but none of them ever came for a visit during working hours. I was so lonely it didn't matter that he wouldn't have time to chat. I was so self-centered, I didn't consider anyone else.

If anybody seemed concerned about my welfare, I pulled away too proud to admit I needed help. I began to spend more time alone.

Terribly restless, unable to sleep at night, I spent the time fastidiously cleaning, but throughout the day I'd collapse into a deep sleep. I became easily irritated and cried a lot when alone.

Although I had no desire to get out of the house, Mom insisted that I join her for every church service. It was useless to protest. I was astute at going through the motions. I knew how to smile, always pretending everything was fine, even though I was smothered with shame. I tried to act normal around others, which meant being someone they wanted me to be. I knew they wouldn't understand the "voice."

My mom had been telling my sister about my new attitude and behavior. She and her husband lived in Oklahoma then. Both were working and finishing their college hours for graduation. She told Mom, "Why don't you bring Ann to spend a week with us. The change might be good for her."

We got there on a weekend so Mom could spend time with Jean and we could see their new little house. I was so jealous of what my sister had. Although her house was small, she still had her husband with her while earning a college degree. She seemed so competent, while I felt so helpless.

Jean and Mom spent most of the weekend getting

caught up on conversation. They had always been close friends. Mom told her things no child should know about their parent's relationship, such as, Dad's infidelity and alcoholism. I guess she needed to justify her reasons for constantly nagging and manipulating him to do things her way.

When Mom left me there and went back home, Jean saw the changes in me that had become evident to my mom.

We stayed in the guest bedroom, but I wasn't sleeping well at all. Adam woke for his 2 am feeding, crying. I quickly changed his diaper, then slipped into the kitchen, warmed his bottle, fed and burped him. Apparently, he had colic and continued crying. The more he cried, the more frustrated I became. I didn't know how to deal with colic, so I decided to ignore him. I laid him on the bed and walked out, closing the door behind me. Tuning out his crying, I decided to surprise my sis and husband with breakfast. It never occurred to me they wouldn't appreciate breakfast at 3 am!

Jean told me later they kept waiting for me to tend to Adam. When I didn't, she went into the room and picked him up. She smelled the bacon frying and found me cheerfully setting the table for breakfast. I remember how disappointed I was when she said, "Ann, it's really too early for us to eat.
Adam is asleep now. Why don't you go back to bed and we'll eat breakfast when we get up in a few hours?" Then she patted my arm and wearily went back to bed. None of this seemed unusual to me but highly out of order for others.

I am sure Jean and Mom discussed my behavior and thought something should be done, but there finally came a point that determined my internment in a mental institution.

Chapter 3: Others Notice Change

Kathy was my neighbor when I was nine years old. She had no siblings. Overweight, adopted and spoiled, she was the only kid I knew who wore corrective shoes; the kind that looked like grandma's lace up ankle boots with steel toes...ugly. She hated them, but learned to hurt you with them if you scuffled with her. She also wore braces on her teeth. Nobody wore braces then, but Kathy's parents gave her anything they thought would enrich her life. They didn't know that some things would cause her to be different from most kids and thereby rejected.

She came to play every day at our house. Her idea of play was awry. We played whatever she wanted to play. If you won at games, she got mad and said you were cheating, tossed the board game from the table and stomped home. Little by little, she learned to give some, if she didn't want to be lonely. She was especially jealous of my time. I tolerated her possessiveness. She was the only girl my age in our neighborhood and her mom made great pimento cheese sandwiches.

We remained close friends until junior high, but then followed other interests. We slowly saw less and less of each other and enjoyed different social groups.

Kathy matured and went to college. She was home for the weekend and wanted to visit. She brought a gift for the baby and decided to pop in late one afternoon.

I was surprised by the knock on my door. I opened it and peeped out.

"Hi, Ann," She reached through the door and around me with a hug, holding a wrapped gift, her purse strap over her shoulder. "Your Mom told me where you were living and said it would be all right to come over. Are you surprised?"

Yes, I was surprised. Not only because of her unannounced visit, but Kathy had lost a lot of weight, dyed her hair blonde and looked adorable!
She sported a perfect "flip" complete with headband that matched a starched cotton blouse, tucked into a slim straight skirt that made her hips look narrow. I

was instantly impressed…and envious. She looked like a model for Seventeen.

My dowdy house dress was rumpled and faded. With fuzzy house shoes and no makeup, and my hair uncombed, I mumbled excuses for the way I looked as she talked non-stop.

"I hope I didn't come at a bad time. I heard you had the baby and wanted to see him. Is he asleep?" She seemed so carefree, so happy and alert looking past my shoulder to get a glimpse of Adam.

She rattled on about being busy at Baylor University. Her social life was as bubbly as a hot kettle of tea, while mine seemed stale as crackers in the back of a dark pantry.

"Can I see him?" she asked.

We tip-toed to the crib and I listened while she cooed well wishes and talked about her semester at school. She was a real "Chatty Kathy". My mind wandered while she talked.

Eventually she asked, "How are you doing? Don't you miss Jeff a lot? What do you do all day?"

This gave me an opportunity to tell her how things were. At last, I had someone who would listen.

I began erupting like a volcano. "Things are okay, I guess. It is so boring and lonesome. Every day I do the same things over and over. I really miss school, all my friends, and people my own age. I wish Jeff was here and we had a life together. He writes often, but he doesn't have to deal with this. I hate being alone. I'm married but don't feel like it with him so far away. I have all this responsibility with the baby, but nobody to help. Mom said we could live with her, but I hate the way she took over the baby as soon as I brought him home from the hospital. I couldn't do anything right. Of course, that's nothing new. You know how she is. I never could please her. It's so hard to be married and still under her control. She's such a perfectionist. That's why I moved out. I just couldn't stand it any longer."

And then, because Kathy seemed really interested I

wondered. *Do I dare tell her about the "angel"? Would she understand?* I ventured further. "I had an interesting thing happen to me recently."

She leaned forward, encouraging the story. As I talked, I watched her face for signs of disbelief or shock. There were none. So, I told it all.

"It was such an unusual experience…something special. I hope you understand I'm not making this up. It happened. I can't explain it, but it was real. You are the first to know. I could never tell Mom. She would not believe it was true.

Kathy never revealed any change in her perception of me. Instead, she stood and hugged me again before she left. I trusted that I had convinced her of my commission. I felt as though my "angel experience" was verified. She didn't think it strange, or at least, she didn't say.

In truth, Kathy had been very alarmed by my behavior and the vision I had. She immediately called her mother, Lucille, and told her what I'd said and how strange I'd acted.

Kathy's mom was a nurse for a prominent doctor in town and called my Mom. She soon arrived to the point of her call.

"I'm worried about Ann." she said. "Kathy just came from a visit with her, and Ann told her some really disturbing things. Ann thinks she saw an angel. She also said she was feeling lonely and hated being married. Do you know anything about this? Lately, has she seemed strange?"

I imagine my mom said something like this. "No, Lucille. She's been taking care of the baby and doing fine. I can't imagine her saying any of those things to Kathy. I thought it was a big mistake for her to move out. Now, she probably realizes I was right. I'll check on her though. Thanks for telling me." Mom hated others to know our family secrets.

Lucille wisely advised Mom to contact the doctor on base and set up a meeting with a psychiatrist. She suspected post partum psychosis.

Instead, Mom called our local MD and set up a time with him.

The next day the three of us sat in the doctor's office and "talked." They shared things about me as if I weren't in the room and I kept my mouth shut. I had learned a big lesson. Don't trust anybody with my story.

Welding her authority, Mom said. "Go sit in the lobby, Ann, while I talk to the doctor a few more minutes."

I obeyed, but thought to myself, *"If they can keep secrets from me, I can keep secrets of my own!"*

Nothing more was said about the angel, at least not for a few more days.

Chapter 4: Sick Mind

A week later, Mom drove me to the base hospital for an appointment. I didn't know what to expect, and frankly, I didn't care.

We sat in the waiting room, Mom holding the baby as I sat by her side, the other "child." I felt so caged, so lifeless. It seemed hours before I saw the doctor. It didn't matter. I was going to see a doctor whether I wanted to or not.

After I endured the post partum physical, he asked. "Are you getting plenty of rest between caring for the baby? Are you eating well? Still taking your vitamins?"

I lied to him. "Yes, I feel fine. I'm working on losing weight but I'm eating meals as usual. I'm a little tired. I'm up in the night feeding the baby, but I nap in the afternoon when he is sleeping. "

He wrote a few notes, then, he asked me if I would talk to another doctor.

Not suspecting anything, I agreed.

A few minutes later, the other doctor came through the door. He extended his hand introducing himself while pumping mine, brandishing a smile as big as a quarter-moon. He said he wanted to know more about me.

"What are you doing to keep yourself busy now that you and the baby are getting to know each other?"

What a dope! What does he think I'm doing on $85.00 per month…taking scuba lessons?

I answered meekly. "Oh, I'm just trying to be a good mom. Staying home, keeping the bottles and diapers clean, doing what everybody does at home… the usual stuff."

The truth was I'd lost interest in almost everything. I'd been an avid reader, yet it had been months since I read anything. I couldn't focus for very long. My mind wandered.

My voice changed, too. I was a high soprano in high school and won the most prestigious awards given in interscholastic competitions. In fact, my vocal abilities gave me opportunities for scholarships from all over the nation. Julliard, in New York, had been one of the invitations I had received. Now I owned a singing voice entirely foreign to me, like a growling tuba. I guessed it was hormone changes...or punishment from God.

The doctor became a little more inquisitive. "Your mother told me you had a very special dream. Do you want to tell me about it?"

To stall for time and decide whether I could trust my story with the doctor, I ventured, "What dream are you talking about?" I didn't fully trust the path he was taking.

"You know...the one with the angel. What did he look like? Have you seen him again? Did he say anything to you? I have a real interest in angelic beings. They're like ghosts. Some say they don't exist. I'd like to know."

The questions came in rapid fire. Should I trust him? Does he really have an interest in what I saw?

I listened for the "voice" to tell me what to do. Silence. So, I decided to tell the doctor exactly what had happened as best I remembered. It was still invigorating to relive the moment. If others didn't believe, at least I did. The angel chose me to be faithful to him. I refused to hide that fact any longer. It happened and I was not ashamed to tell it.

The doctor listened patiently as he scribbled notes. It never occurred to me how much power he had. He was about to change my life. I never saw it coming, but then, no one who is abnormal ever believes they are so. I thought I was "special" and everyone else was marching in the wrong direction...but not me!

You may say all this took place in my mind...and in some ways, it did. But the vision was so real that the subsequent six months in a mental hospital and fourteen shock treatments never dissipated it from my mind. I lost a lot of other memories permanently...but not that one.

PART II

THE INTERNMENT

Chapter 5: Inside the Asylum

Terrell State Mental Hospital stretched like a sleeping cat atop a gentle hill away from the busy main street. The grounds were enclosed with a low brick wall and opened iron gates. Like the "yellow brick road," a concrete driveway led to the main admissions building. It was obvious that effort was made to make the facility seem restful and inviting.

I was curious but not frightened. I was accustomed to feeling powerless and inferior. This wasn't the first time, and it wouldn't be the last.

Mom parked the car and we unloaded the few items I was allowed.
I had enough clothes for seven days and a few other items. I was not allowed a mirror, deodorant, nail file or polish remover. Precautions were taken against suicide. I guess it was an assumption that all patients had a "death wish."

I held my baby, twiddling with little fingers and toes, while Mother signed the official papers. I pretended to be aloof from all the procedures, letting my eyes rove around the room, listening intensely to the conversation. They decided for six weeks I would have days uncluttered with responsibility, and given meds to calm my emotional state brought on by hormonal changes in my body. They thought I suffered from post partum psychosis. None of us knew I would be staying much longer when other events unfolded.

I felt smothered by control and hardly concealed the anger I felt.

I was really anxious to get on with a new life...even though it began at a "funny farm."

Then Mom took Adam from my arms and yielded me to my "handlers." Over my shoulder I watched the two of them leave my life. Instantly, I felt the freedom from it all. *No more control and no more responsibility! This may not be so bad after all. At least now I can be who I want to be without shame, resentment, or obligation. I can be free!*

The attendant ushered me past the admittance office down a long corridor.
I was shown the cafeteria, library, craft room and recreation area. Finally, I came to my dorm area.

Ward B was a large, open room with areas separated by half walls of concrete blocks. Each area enclosed eight iron hospital beds with a metal nightstand beside each. A box under the bed was my closet. Everything looked like soldiers…neat and organized, not like my Mom's house.

Inside the large room was the nurses' station. It was a concrete- block cubicle with heavy plate glass windows, a safe place for the nurses to monitor our every move. Three times a day we were called to the station and administered our medications. We also lined up there for meals and other scheduled activities. We were escorted everywhere. No one went anywhere unmonitored.

We had three meals a day in the cafeteria as well as craft time, library visits, and plenty of free time in the recreation room. This was where all the patients mingled for socialization, playing cards, ping pong or billiards.

We were an odd mix of people of different ages and varied walks of life.
Gwendolyn smoked incessantly, never smiled, and hated her husband.
Guy and Donald, our two gay residents, were the life of the party, always joking, making crude remarks and sneaking to the restroom for illicit recreation. Ben was a tall, handsome brute but very reclusive. I'd see him in the corner, a frown on his face, watching everyone but never getting involved. Mrs. Weaver talked a lot. She was lonesome and made up for her emptiness by filling every silent space with words. She never realized how quickly we tired of her chatter and tuned her out completely. It didn't matter. She kept talking anyway.

I was the youngest of our group. We were all there for one reason. We didn't belong with normal people. The stigma of being committed to a mental institution in the '60's had not lost its edge from the Dark Ages.

We all felt incompetent, weak, and labeled "freaks." Though none of this was ever said to our faces, in our former lives we joked of being "sent to Terrell" if we socially stepped out of line. So, now we knew how it felt to be the brunt of all those jokes.

After lunch, we had an hour to rest on our beds. I soon realized my sleeping habits were about to change. I could no longer stay awake at night and sleep in the daytime.

We were kept occupied outside the dorm most of the day. Once per week we had some entertainment...a movie, an ice cream social, a dance, a speaker, and of course, we also attended group therapy led by the "shrink-of-the-day."

Group therapy was a meeting in a small room with one of the doctors who asked questions and we answered...or not. It went something like this:

Doctor: "Why do you think you are here?"

Patients: (Silence)

Doctor: "Okay. I'll ask another question. Do you think it is fair that you are here?"

Patients: (Silence)

Doctor: "Ben...would you like to answer that question?"

Ben: (shrug of shoulders.....silence)

So, it went for thirty minutes. We never talked while the doctor scribbled a few notes on his clipboard and usually closed the session early to go have a cigarette. Case closed.

None of us felt we were supposed to be there. We just accommodated our families or whoever had us committed for treatment. It was an understood tolerance. If we lasted the duration, we were free to go home or elsewhere with a clean slate saying we were cured, but records showed forever we had once had a mental disorder.

It was in Terrell State Mental Hospital I had my first

taste of liquor, my first cigarette, and my first dance, as none of these were allowed under my mother's rules.

Gwendolyn always carried a flask of whiskey and a can of Coke with her. When she finished the Coke, she filled the can with liquor. She convinced me I should at least have a taste. They all laughed as I experienced the "burn" when I swallowed some.

She also supplied my first cigarette. We played Canasta several hours a day and smoking was allowed in the recreation room. She kept plying me with cigs until I realized I was beginning to enjoy the taste. Then I decided smoking was a habit I didn't want and stopped.

Having the freedom to make choices made me feel powerful. I never considered I had personal responsibility in doing so. After all, my Mom and sister had always cleaned up my messes, albeit they grumbled as they did the favor. For years, I used the "dummy" card whenever I failed.

Chapter 6: The Escape

Bob began hanging around our group not long after he arrived. He was in his early 30's, balding, and "street wise." He was wiry and wild and soon was particularly interested in me. I was too unaware to know he had a plan in mind.

One day he told me, "You know, we could leave this place anytime we want." That thought had never entered my mind. "These doors aren't locked and neither are the gates out front. All we have to do is walk out. But we need some money to take a bus to Dallas after we get out of here. Do you have any?"

I started to tell him that I had none, but then the "voice" spoke. "Ann, you can get money from Mrs. Weaver. She has lots of money. Simply ask her for some."

I turned to Bob and asked, "How much money?"

"Oh," he said, "I think $15 would be enough to get us both tickets."

I thought. *Do I dare go against the rules and just boldly walk off the grounds?* Immediately the "voice" reminded me that I was on a mission and leaving Terrell was just a part of getting where I needed to be. Rising from the couch I said, "Wait here, Bob. I'll see what I can do."

I found Mrs. Weaver in her cubicle and sat down beside her. Eager to have a listener, she began her one- way conversation. When she stopped for a breath, I assumed a pitiful countenance and blurted out, "Mrs. Weaver, I'm in trouble."

Immediately I had her attention. Her face wrinkled into concern. After a pause, she patted my hand and said, "Well, dear, you can tell me anything. Your secret is safe with me."

Yeah, about as safe as a blind man in the middle of a four- lane highway!

"I think I'm pregnant," I said. "I need to go to a doctor and get tested but I don't have any money."

I knew it was a blatant lie, but by this time I believed nothing was wrong if it benefitted the new plan for my life. This was another test to see if the "voice" was still right. *Would I get the money?*

I watched her as she dug her billfold from her purse. Then she turned and asked, "How much do you need, sweetie?" She held out a stack of money as casually as if I'd asked her for a Kleenex.

I ducked my head (pretending shame) and said, "It shouldn't cost very much…maybe $15?"

It never occurred to me to ask for more. Money was always "tight" at our house and Mom choked the purse strings till they turned blue. So, I always asked for the minimum I thought I could get.

Mrs. Weaver thrust the bills into my hand, leaning in intimately, whispering, "Now you come back and tell me what the doctor says. Okay?"

"Oh, I promise I will," I said, playing the "poor-little-girl-in-trouble."

I even thanked her with a hug of gratitude. As I turned my back, a smug smile spread over my face. I had gotten what I asked for. *It takes so little faith to move mountains now.*

Like a child sent on an errand, I almost skipped back into the recreation room and handed the money to Bob. His face lit up with surprise.

"Well, that didn't take long. Where did you get it?" he asked.

"From Mrs. Weaver," I answered. "She's loaded with money. I told her I thought I was pregnant and needed money to get tested. She just gave it to me. It was easy. What's next?"

Bob stretched his leg away from the couch as he stuffed the money into his jeans and said, "Now we wait 'til supper call and walk out the front gates."

"But won't somebody see us leaving?" I asked, still piqued by concern that authority was always watching.

"Naw," he said with a sniff, "We'll just get at the end of the line and slip out as the nurse turns the corner toward the cafeteria. By the time we are missed, we'll be on the bus headed to Dallas."

So that's exactly what we did. It never occurred to me that anything harmful could happen should I make that choice. I had no moorings in my new life. It seemed I didn't make choices. I just lived with whatever came at the moment. No choices…no consequences. At least, that was my opinion at the time.

Chapter 7: Lost in Dallas

We left the grounds about 4:30 that afternoon. Texas heat in summer was like stepping into a sauna with faulty heat controls. By the time we walked a few blocks to the bus station, my clothes were drenched in sweat.

I brought nothing but the clothes I wore. That didn't seem important at the time. The new venture had begun.

We got off the bus in Dallas and left the station. The sidewalks swarmed with people getting off work. Bumping against the flow, Bob cautioned me to keep close as we darted across the street into the shade of tall buildings.

A few blocks down, we entered a shabby hotel.

"We'll stay here for the night and find a cheaper place tomorrow." Bob said.

The floors were old, made of two- inch octagonal black and white tile. It was relatively clean, but not maintained. Baseboards and doors bubbled with darkened varnish from years past. Light fixtures were white milk glass bowls that hung from ornate black chains. The place had the smell of old, wet wood.

We stepped into a wire-front elevator cage opened by an old black man with bloodshot eyes and stooped shoulders.

"Floor sir?" he asked, his head bowed.

"Two," Bob replied.
I wasn't paying much attention to anything but my surroundings. I'd been in an elevator only a few times in my life and never in one that didn't have a solid door.

We stepped off the elevator at the end of a long hallway that echoed. The same black and white tile formed the barren path. It seemed we were the only people in the whole place, though I later heard voices outside our room.

The walls were thin plaster with high ceilings and old, sparse furnishings. There was one iron bed, painted white. White sheets were atop the well-worn mattress. No blanket...two pillows. I wondered if we would share the bed but shelved that thought for awhile.

A white porcelain sink was in the corner, pipes disappearing into the wall, held it in place. The toilets and showers were down the hall. I couldn't wait to get cleaned up. I was hot, tired and thirsty.

Bob turned and said, "Wait here. I'll go find us something to eat."
While he was gone, I drank tepid water at the sink from my cupped hands then wiped the sticky sweat off my body with a thin white washcloth. Suddenly, my wedding band slipped off my finger and down the sink drain. I had lost so much weight by not eating much, it twirled loosely most of the time. My reaction to its loss was nonchalant.

Oh, well, in my new life, I won't need it anymore.

By the time Bob returned to the room, I was already asleep.

Chapter 8: Rock Bottom

The next morning, I woke to the tune of honking cars, diesel buses, and toilets flushing down the hall. Bob was already up and dressed.

He rushed me saying, "Get up and get going. We've got lots to do and several places to go."

We first entered a bank. He asked me the day we left Terrell if I had any money in the bank at home. I had carefully saved a little over $300 in my home town bank and told him so. Now, he said we needed that money to get to Brazil. I was so naïve, it never occurred to me I was being conned. I never even asked him why we were going to Brazil.

In those days, it was easy to transfer money from one bank to another.
All banks had impersonal, blank checks provided on marble counters for public use. You simply wrote in the amount you wished to transfer, signed the check and took it to a teller, who verified by phone the money was available and had it transferred. You

didn't have to prove identity. In general then, we had a moral culture that seldom considered deceit in such a way. To be asked for verification of identity was almost non-existent.

I could not remember what my name was on our account. *Was it Ann Norris or Ann Martin Norris?*

In my confused state, I didn't remember how to sign the check. I decided on the latter, signed quickly, and handed the check to the teller. A few moments later, she returned and asked, "How can I contact you when the money transfers…a phone number or address?"

Pushing me aside, Bob stepped quickly to the cage front and said, "We'll call you. We just got into town and don't have a phone. We'll locate an apartment today and then call you with a number."

Hurriedly, I was ushered away from the teller and back out on the streets.
His reluctance to allow me to talk to the teller didn't seem strange.
 I was accustomed to having others talk for me all my

life.

It seemed we walked around Dallas for hours. We stopped once at an open-air shop on a corner. Bob told me to sit at the counter and have some ice cream while he talked to a man nearby. Like a three year old, I obeyed everything he told me to do. The ice cream was cold and sweet and I was hungry. I licked my lips slowly to make it last. Soon, he returned and told me he had found a place we could stay.

We caught a bus and rode several blocks to a run-down old house with a broken porch on Junius Street. It wore peeling paint like an old lady wears orange make up and dyed hair. The house was one of many turn-of the-century houses near downtown. It was worn out and far less attractive than its original condition. The occupants resembled the same description, but I was tired and trusted the "voice" knew what was best for me. Bob gave the woman fifty cents for the night, and we moved in.

I was ready for some rest. My periods of being really sleepy were coming back. It was all I could do to keep my eyes open and my mind focused.

Other voices filled my brain, murmurings similar to voices you'd hear in a dentist chair as you are given the "relaxing gas"...distant and indistinct.

All I wanted was a place to lie down and take a nap. It was as if my body and mind were not connected. I could "check out" of reality anytime I wanted. I would just sleep.

The next memories I have are in segments of happenings. I don't remember all that occurred in the three days I was missing from Terrell, but I retained a few instances. I don't know whether they were true incidences, or were imagined in my sick mind. They seemed real enough to recall, if not connected in sequence.

One memory I have is being in the room at night, and a single, bare light bulb hanging from a long cord in the ceiling. I was on a dirty mattress in the middle of the room on an unvarnished wooden floor with several men standing over me; some were Mexican and some were white. They sneered and grabbed for my legs and arms, circling me as I twirled my body to face them all.

At some point in that experience, I realized to survive I must become a tiger. It was like a dream (or an act). I fought off the men as best I could. I clawed, snarled, bit and screeched as if I was a real tiger. Then, I remember nothing else. I didn't realize until much later that Bob was probably being a "pimp" while I was eating ice cream, but none of this could be proven for a court case.

Another time, I stood on the porch with Bob and the landlady. He told her we expected a call from the bank and asked her to let him know immediately when the bank called. While they talked, the thought entered my mind to run away. I was tired of Bob's control and wanted my freedom.
better stop running, you bitch!"

I stepped off the porch and ran fast down the sidewalk. In the background, I could hear him calling me. "What the hell are you doing? Hey! Come back here! You bitch!"

He was fast catching up with me when I spied a small

alcove under a wooden staircase on a house nearby. It was covered with vines, so I darted inside.

While trying to hold my breath, thinking he wouldn't find me, a woman in an apartment at the top of the stairs stuck her head out the rusty screen door and caught my attention.

"Pssst...come up here, Honey. Hurry! He can't get you here," she coaxed.
I don't know why her urgent demand caused me to click into reality for a moment. Maybe I feared Bob's reprisal if I didn't stop running, but for whatever reason, I stepped out of the alcove laughing and pretending it was all a joke.

Bob grabbed my elbow and through clenched teeth spewed, "Where do you think you are going? You won't last ten minutes on these streets without me! Now I'll have to keep you here 'til the bank calls."

With that, he took me back to the room and locked me inside. The door had an old fashioned lock that kept the door secure from both sides. It couldn't be opened without the key, and he took the key with him.

The day grew hotter in the house. It was not air conditioned, so I pulled the bed closer to a tall open window. I took off all my clothes except my underwear and slip and laid down in a fetal position to sleep.

After a while, a tall young man wearing a white shirt, black slacks and a thin, black tie shook me awake. He held my shoulder gently and explained,
"Ann, everything is going to be all right. Don't be afraid. I'm Camille's friend."

I had sung in a high school trio with Camille. I don't remember that I grabbed his wrist and pleaded, "Don't let them hurt me anymore!" but I was told later that was what I did.

Moments later, the police came into the room. Behind them was my dad.

Chapter 9: Needle in a Haystack

I had no idea how my family found me, a "needle in a haystack", in Dallas for three days. I was told later this is what transpired:

The morning after Bob and I left Terrell, the president of the hospital called my parents and told them I was missing. I never showed up for roll call the night before. Of course, my parents were panic stricken.

When they asked where I was, they were told, "We don't know exactly.
She was not seen here after six o'clock last night when the staff noticed her missing. We began a search throughout the grounds but didn't find her."

The president reminded them of the waiver they signed that the hospital would not be held accountable should I leave the premises without their knowledge.

My dad was furious that I had not been watched more carefully. Legally, my parents didn't have rights to any information the hospital had about my disappearance.

Dad was tenacious. When he suspected you had more information, he had ways of getting it from you. So, he dressed in his best suit and necktie, drove to Terrell that day and asked to speak to the president of the hospital about my absence. He was ushered into the president's office and treated sensitively because it wasn't often the institution had to admit they couldn't keep up with their patients all the time.

My dad was always direct. He got to the point early in their conversation.
"Thank you for seeing me, Dr._____. We have been worried sick about our daughter since your call. I've hired a detective to find her but we need a few details about her leaving. Do you know if she was alone when she left, or with someone else? Did anyone else go missing about the same time?"

The president dropped his head and stroked his chin before answering.
"We did have one other patient missing," he said,

looking over the rim of his glasses, "but I cannot divulge that information. Patient's rights, you know."

The answer he gave was insufficient for my father. He knew the guy had a lead and wasn't going to let it go. Before the meeting was over, my dad told the president he was going to sit at his office door morning and night until he had the information he wanted…which was the name of the person who went missing with me. So, I guess with that proclamation, he was told about "Bob", which wasn't his real name.

Bob was committed to Terrell by the courts. He had a criminal past and was there for the duration of rehabilitation. I suppose the president weighed the cost of his own ethics of strictly adhering to policy against the importance of Bob's privacy. So with the information he came for, Dad left. In the meantime the check that I had written was sent to my bank at home.

Now, I don't know if you believe in "fate" or "divine intervention," but I think the latter happened because my religious mother was praying like
Daniel- in- the- lion's- den about this time. She fasted

and prayed from the time they were told I was missing until I was found. I know for all the "living by the law" she did...she still had a heart that loved me. She just never knew how to express it in a way I understood.

For whatever reason, the check arrived at the bank and landed on the desk of my sister-in-law who worked there. When she opened the transfer and saw my name on the check, she immediately called Mom and gave her the address of our location. It was a little over an hour after that, I was found.

Dad rode to Dallas with the police and was there when they confronted "Bob" about me. At first he denied he had had anything to do with me. He knew he would either go back to jail or back to Terrell for his escape, but he didn't want any more charges against him so he lied about my being behind the locked door. After a little bit of 60's "police persuasion" I imagine they permitted my dad to "convince" the guy to unlock the door. It was then the detective with the white shirt and tie walked in and found me on the bed.

They took me immediately to a doctor for a pelvic

examination to find evidence of rape. Without the discovery of DNA at that time, they had none. Other than the bruises inside my thighs and around my throat, they had no way to convict "Bob" of rape or forced prostitution, so they loaded my dad and me in the back seat of the squad car and got a court order for me to be re-committed to Terrell State Mental Institution in "locked" ward. I would not get out a second time.

I have one sweet memory of that ride in the squad car. I had dysentery and threw up on the floor of the car, then rested with my head in my dad's lap. He patted my hand and said, "I love you, honey." My dad had never told me he loved me before. To this day, I cry to think of it. I had longed for that moment all my life.

Chapter 10: Locked Ward

We arrived at Terrell late afternoon. Again, I was ushered through those doors, but this time to a different area altogether.

I must have been acting violently because they placed me in a padded cell. It was a concrete block cubicle, like a jail cell, with one small, barred window on the back wall. A single light bulb perched in the ceiling. All the walls were covered with gym mats. I guess some patients might kill themselves by banging their head against the wall. The room had a drain in the middle of the floor I suppose to allow defecation and urination? The only door was very thick with a small window through which I could be observed. I don't remember ever getting out of the cell until they deemed me calmed down enough to join others. An attendant brought all my meals and re-sedated me each time he entered the room. I just slept most of the time until I was released to a regular dorm room.

The facilities seemed the same with one major difference. Heavy metal doors with large chains and padlocks were on every outside wall. Our walking area was a rectangle of dead grass the size of a driveway surrounded by a tall concrete block wall.

When ushered outside for exercise, most of us stayed on the covered porch out of the sun, trying to breathe for the duration. We were never allowed to go anywhere without several attendants escorting us. The clientele in the locked wards were more visibly insane than those in unlocked ward.

Some walked as if there were magnets in their shoes sticking them to the floor. Chins down, blank stares, drooling and social isolation were common traits of my new roommates. One old woman whispered conversations to imaginary people continuously. Even after "lights out" she whistled like a tea kettle on into the night. I learned to tune her out just to be able to sleep.

A stark difference in treatment came a few days later. I was on my bed sorting through some things in my cubicle when the nurse at the station called out names to go somewhere. I had noticed this procedure previously, but never questioned where the patients were taken. I found it interesting, however, that several of them begged not to go and all of them came back about an hour later either transported in wheelchairs or helped along by an orderly back to their beds. I wasn't concerned until they called my name.

There must be some mistake. They never called my name before. I'll just speak with the head nurse and get this mistake corrected.

She would not talk to me. She checked her chart and barked, "Get in line with the others and do as you are told!"

When we were all in line, they marched us out of our ward through a long passageway into another building. As we approached the door to one designated room, I saw blue light flashing and heard the whirring of electric current periodically turned on and off. Without the permission to talk, I didn't expect what was soon to happen.

I don't think I had heard of "shock treatments" before, so at that moment I experienced the panic of what it might feel like waiting in line to be thrown into a venomous snake pit. My mouth went dry. I shivered with cold and tried to keep from crying. My mind raced with questions. *Is this a torture room? What's going on in there?*

Some of the patients quietly sniffled, chewed their nails or twisted their hands. Most of us just leaned into the wall and waited. We were told not to talk to each other. Keep quiet and wait in line. As usual, I did what I was told when I felt threatened.

Then it came my turn to enter the room. Inside, there were three gurneys with white hospital curtains surrounding them. Doctors and nurses attended each bed. There were drip I-V machines beside each bed and other wires all over the floor around them. A metal box that had several switches and a needle-dial gauge sat nearby on a rolling stand. I was told to hop onto one of the gurneys, and the curtains were closed.

All the doctors wore surgical masks and gloves. My arms and legs were strapped to the table and a hard rubber mouth guard was wedged between my teeth.

The anesthesiologist explained that he was going to give me some Sodium Pentothal to put me to sleep, and then I would be given a small electrical shock from the diodes they placed on my temples. It was supposed to help me get well. He said I wouldn't feel anything and I'd probably wake up in my bed back in my ward.

I stretched out my right arm for the procedure. As the needle went in, I tasted a cold, metallic sensation at the back of my throat. Then it seemed my body began floating, and I passed out.

Before I completed the series of fourteen treatments during my stay, I began to look forward to the "sleep" only the medication gave.
It was total and complete rest…something I hadn't experienced in a long time. Artificial sleep was such ecstasy!

I woke up in my bed with an excruciating headache. It seemed my temples would burst open if I moved. Managing to get to the nurses' station, I was given a couple of aspirin that helped some. With each treatment, the headaches lessened.

I never reached the point of calm each time we stood in that hall outside the shock room, but I knew it would be over soon, and I'd get to sleep all day if I wanted to.

Later, after my release from Terrell, my parents told me they had to sign a release the hospital required to administer shock treatments. The hospital would not be held accountable should I die on that treatment table.

Shock treatments were reserved for patients who didn't seem to improve from conventional healing methods. Experimental methods were always risky and some patients never recovered from the "scrambling" of their brains. Some even died in the process.

I had only one experience when the dosage of Sodium Pentothal wasn't as effective as usual.

I crawled up onto the gurney. They strapped my arms down, placed the hard rubber device in my mouth and began the IV drip. I heard the attendant say, "She's out now. Go ahead." But I wasn't! I can still remember the panic I felt...like being in a dream trying to run away from danger but unable to move. Then I blacked out.

After the shock treatments, I was less angry. In fact, I had no emotions at all. I felt nothing. I said little and went about the routine like a zombie. It also could have been all the intensive medication they were trying.

Nevertheless, Dr. Sandoz, my new doctor, told my parents I would never recover unless my husband was released from military duty and provided a normal home life for me. He classified me as "severe paranoid schizophrenic." Not good.

Most people I know today would never in a million

years suspect I was once mentally, emotionally, and socially challenged. They usually recoil in surprise and think I am joking when I tell them I spent an extended time in a mental institution. How I healed is the rest of my story.

PART III

THE HEALING DAYS

Chapter 11: Released

Jeff was granted an honorable hardship discharge from the Air Force and came home. He had been far removed from all the drama that was going on in our families. His mom had been advised by my doctor in Terrell to take baby Adam and keep him until further notified, which infuriated Mom.

She had also been restricted from visiting me. The doctor must have picked up on all my anger toward her.

So, when Jeff arrived back home from overseas, he was instantly advised by his family to divorce me. They were eager to be rid of me and help Jeff raise our baby without a "crazy" mother involved. I can't say that I blame them, but they didn't know the entire story.

I must say that my husband loved me more than anyone else could. I'm sure there were days when he questioned whether his decision to stay with me was best.

He went to our church pastor for advice after hearing all the tales of my escape from Terrell and all my other sordid escapades. Our wise pastor told Jeff to stay with me and together raise our baby. He believed that God's original plan for marriage was for a lifetime...for better or worse. We were introduced to the "worse" part early in our marriage.

"Stay with her, Jeff," he advised. "She needs you now more than ever. God will bless you if you keep your promise to love and cherish her." With that encouragement, my husband rented a little house. I was released to his care and we began a new life together.

I wish I could say that instantly all the problems went away. But it takes a long time to untangle a wad of knotted string...and that's exactly what my life was like at the time. I hated myself and what I had become. I still didn't adjust to responsibility and was bored with the daily chores of caring for a baby and husband. I still had dreams of being independent someday. Jeff had his hands full, but his love remained constant when mine was non-existent, or at best, weak and self-seeking.

I made the decision a few weeks later to flush all my medication down the toilet. I reasoned I would probably be dependent on it for the rest of my life, and loathed the way it made me feel. I was sluggish all the time. It seemed I never got enough sleep, even though I napped every time Adam did and slept all through the night too. I was probably sleeping as much time as I was awake. Without the drugs, I was forced to cope with reality. I told no one that I had dumped them.

My emotions were raw. When I was depressed, I cried all day. When I was angry, I lashed out at anything and anyone around me. I had no joy at that time. What was there to be happy about? Most of my days were spent in dull routine. I just made myself take one step at a time, waiting for some miracle to happen that would remove me from my prison. I had no idea that a lot of people in the world lived the same way…dull routine, day after day, with no hope for the future. Self-pity engulfed me.

Weeks passed by. It was fall, and I had no car. I was getting restless with the routine of living...washing bottles and diapers, cooking every day. I wanted to get away from the heaviness I felt of all work and no play. We didn't have money to do anything outside of surviving.

One day I decided to bundle up baby Adam, tuck him in his stroller and walk ten blocks to our public library. At least walking and books at the library were free. Because it had been so long since I made a simple decision of my own, I felt frightened. At the same time, I felt I'd burst if I didn't break the boredom.

It felt good to be outside. The wind was crisp, so I just walked faster to keep warm and keep the fear at bay. I felt like a caged animal that had discovered the door was open...reluctant at first, afraid I might be punished for trying something new, gradually running with the excitement of having some freedom. Soon, I was on my way back home and the warmth of the gas space heater, proud of my accomplishment. The stroller rack was loaded with picture books for the baby and several novels of my own. I felt a fresh upsurge of energy that I hadn't felt in a long time...and a glimmer of self-confidence.

That night, after supper, Jeff and I sat in the bed with Adam between us.
We read to him, making the noises of young parents, pointing to the pictures of a cow or pig, mooing and grunting in turn. It felt good to laugh again and again each time Adam looked up, his little fat cheeks wadded up in a grin just before he'd squeal with joy at our antics. I'm sure he welcomed the relief that laughter brought to our lives. It had been a long time since any of us had laughed together.

Chapter 12: God's "Voice"

Fall turned into winter and later into the whisper of spring to come. With the changing seasons came change in our lives again. Jeff was laid off from his job.

He came through the door, his lean frame heavy with worry. "Honey, I've got some bad news. I'm out of a job in a week."

We knew the business of airplane manufacturing was "if-y" at best, but the pay was the best in town. The downside was frequent lay-offs.

Jeff took his responsibility of providing for his family seriously. He worried constantly about finding a new job before his pay ran out. We didn't have a dime in savings and moving in with either of our families was not an option. He began looking for an opportunity to work elsewhere.

His supervisor respected Jeff and knew he would be a good employee anywhere. He called him aside and told him, "Jeff, I did some calling yesterday and discovered that our plant in Grand Prairie is hiring now."

He tucked a scrap of paper in my husband's hand and said, "Call this number and ask for Dave. If you don't mind a long commute, the chances are you'll get hired immediately."

Of course, Jeff jumped at the chance. He carried a good recommendation from Dave, was hired, and started driving the following Monday to a new job in Grand Prairie, an hour and half away from home.

He left the house every day long before daylight and didn't come back until after dark. The new plant scheduled him for twelve hour shifts, six days a week. Although he was relieved to have more money coming in, he was drained from all the driving and extra work hours. When he finally got home after the day, all he wanted was a bath, a good meal and bed. Once more I felt I was alone, the same way I felt when he was overseas.

In the meantime, my mom started making daily visits to the house to be certain I was doing all right with the baby. I'm sure she meant well, but I resented her presence and was relieved each time she left. I didn't want her supervision again. I was still swollen with pent up anger and cringed with every attempt she made to give advice or give us money.

As I look back now, I know her heart must have bled each time I curtly refused her help. I wanted to say, "I don't need your advice or help. Can't you see I am capable of functioning without your control?!" I couldn't say those words to her…so I just put my thoughts into actions.

Months passed, with the drive and long hours taking their toll on our family.
Jeff didn't have enough energy left for us after all that work. I missed him terribly and began thinking we needed to move closer to his work. At least he could eliminate four hours a day driving.
When I first suggested my idea of moving, Jeff dug in his heels and firmly refused. He thought that work would soon ease up or he would be called back to his

former job in town.

There's nothing he hated worse than moving. I don't know if all men are like that, or only him. In our entire married life, every time we relocated, he was this way, but with my persistence he gave in and allowed me to start searching for a house near Grand Prairie.

Since Jeff drove our only vehicle to work each day, my mother offered to help find a rent house nearer his job. I took her offer, and we bought a Dallas area paper each week and began the search.

Available rental houses in Dallas in 1968 were sparse in our price range.
We couldn't afford to pay more than $75-$80 per month on housing and survive. Most apartments cost at least $130 per month, and Jeff refused to live in an apartment.

He had been a country boy all his life and felt claustrophobic being squashed into a building shared by hundreds of other people. So, we searched for a house to rent that cost no more than $85 per month.

I wondered at the time if he was just being difficult because he really didn't want to move to Dallas.

Nevertheless, Mom and I drove several weeks to Dallas on a house hunt. In the classifieds, we circled the properties that were in our price range only to find that they were located in high-crime areas, or nearly in ruins. I began to despair, but then our pastor came to the rescue once again. He suggested that we call a fellow pastor he knew in Dallas and get his help.

Reverend Robert Williams was a young, vivacious preacher at a fast growing church in Oak Cliff. He was a ball of energy with a good mind and lots of civic connections. I had known him in my high school years as the director of our church youth camps where I had worked during summers as a teen. He knew Jeff and I would probably be good church members and wanted us in his congregation. It wasn't long until he called back with news of a tentative rent house that might meet our needs.

We drove to Dallas that next weekend and met with the owner. At first he was reluctant to rent to us. He had been painting the house and doing repairs intending to sell it. Obviously, Pastor Robert used his persuasive skills to get the owner to reconsider renting it instead. So, after we looked inside and walked around the house, Jeff agreed. We paid the deposit, were given the keys and began moving in the next week. I was elated!

The house was very small...less than 1,000 square feet, but had a large back yard shaded by a Chinaberry tree. Red roses tumbled thickly over the back fence adding charm. A clothesline was available, and I calculated we could save at least a dollar per week if I used it to dry our laundry.

Our house and all others lining the streets in our neighborhood were government project houses built just after World War II. They all looked alike... small cubicles with a 3'x3' covered porch attached to the front. Built by the returning GI's that flooded the nation after the war needing jobs, they were all rental houses by 1967. I didn't mind. I finally felt I had a place all my own, away from both sets of our parents. I was with the guy I loved and our baby in a house where few people knew us...or our past. The move was good.

We lived there for six years, and in those years I learned to do several things that helped re-build my self-confidence. It was there I first learned the joy of planting a garden and canning the vegetables we harvested. There was something therapeutic in working with my hands.

Somehow, busy hands kept the depression away. It is a coping skill I use today, and it still works.

Other things occupied my mind besides the usual daily chores. I dug out my artist paints and began painting daily. I even sold some of my work. I learned to sew, and it was then I began writing. Once again, I began singing. Jeff and I joined another young couple in a quartet at church.

I discovered when I accomplished things admired by others, my self- esteem flourished. Always pushing for perfection, I wasn't satisfied with mediocre endeavors. It became a habit.

It wasn't long after we moved into that house that our new pastor came for a visit. Apparently he knew of my recent difficulties and wanted to help.
Since we couldn't afford a phone, he came unannounced. I had just laid Adam down for a nap.

I heard the knock on the front door and was surprised to see him there. I put on my best smile and invited him in for a visit.

"Oh, hello, Brother Williams...won't you come in. I just made a fresh pot of coffee."

I was able to pretend everything was fine in my life, hoping with our new location no one would know I'd just been released from an asylum.
He took the coffee and we engaged in small talk for awhile. I never suspected he was a moment away from hitting me between the eyes with truth...and truth was something I hadn't faced for a long time.

In the 50's and 60's, it was common to sugar-coat the outside of your life, hiding the ugly parts under the rug. It was a façade...but one our culture had developed. Socially you didn't talk about the raw parts. He must have not cared for that "rule."

A few minutes later, he cut to the chase. "Ann, how long has it been since you had a good relationship with God?"

My mind sputtered into gear. Should I lie to him and say I was perfectly happy in my spiritual life and nothing was wrong...or tell him the truth? It had been about six years since I'd had a conversation with God at all. Surprising myself, I was honest with him.

"I...it's been a long time, Brother Williams." With that confession I began to cry.

A moment later, he asked if he could pray with me, and as he prayed I realized how much I'd missed having a spiritual connection with God. I felt I was being led into His presence and I had no right to be there.
I was sick of living a sham. I desperately wanted to be genuine, not fake. I wanted to be a good person, but I felt I couldn't be that perfect and I knew

perfection was the standard. Although I desired to talk to God, I didn't feel He would accept me after sinning so much. I thought I had hidden my feelings well. The pastor's confrontation told me I hadn't. Instead, I had deceived myself into thinking no one in those pious circles knew my secret. I went on living as if nothing was wrong, wearing a smile, going to church, toting my Bible under my arm, yet tuning God out of my mind completely, even in church.

For years, I thought freedom lay outside His control. I wanted to make my own choices, do all that seemed right in my own eyes. I was cramped by all the regulations the church and Mom had said were necessary to please God.

Like a wild stallion, I broke down the fences and ran away, but instead of the freedom the "voice" said I would have, I was wrapped in a spider web of self-deceit and lies. The more I struggled, the tighter the web became. I wasn't happy. The joy of more innocent days was gone, and I had no one to blame but myself. I had made some stupid choices and didn't like the consequences.

A few days after the pastor's visit, I was washing dishes, thinking about the broken ties in my spiritual life. Looking back on the past years, I knew exactly when I made the choice to turn away from God and go my own way. I remember the incidents that led to turning my back on Him because I didn't want to "take up the cross" he gave me. I didn't want to deny myself the pleasure of sin.

I still prayed on occasion during that time...whenever I felt I needed His help, or wanted a special favor. The joy of fellowship with Him in a continual way was gone. I had been the one to throw away that relationship...all because of rules. His rules! At that time, I didn't know the rules were there to give me freedom...not to take it away!

I made a commitment to try and mend the gap between God and me.
I came to realize that living a selfish life wasn't as great as I thought. I had no peace in my heart and certainly no self-worth.

So, I prayed "Lord, if you never speak to me again I

will still live my life for you. I will strive to be obedient to all your concepts. I know I don't deserve Your presence in my life, but I will strive to live for you just the same."

I believed the way to do that was to become obedient again. Just going to church regularly didn't meet that need. I knew one thing I should do was study my Bible on a daily basis, so I began spending time each morning alone doing just that. I'd grab my Bible after seeing Jeff out the door and sit on our tiny bathroom floor next to the space heater, reading and meditating

I thought I could just muster the presence of God in my spirit by being obedient, but day after day, my Bible reading was as dull as reading a phone book. Nothing was happening. I wasn't hearing God's voice.

I began to see the seriousness of being angry with God and allowing my selfish nature to control my life. I might never regain the closeness I once had with God and that broke my heart.

I'd known the beauty of constant companionship with

Him. I'd known laughter with Him. I'd cry to Him for help and experience His help almost immediately in every hard situation. It was simply peace to know He was always there for me. He'd been my best friend and loved me whenever I thought no one else did.

While thinking about the possibility that I might have waited too long to return to my heavenly Father, I was guilt-ridden and longed to have God's presence in my life again.

Desperate and full of shame, I prayed this prayer: "Lord, I've made a mess of my life. I know I don't deserve a relationship with You anymore...but if You'll just take me back...I promise to live for You the rest of my life even if I never hear Your "voice" again. I'll still live by your rules. At least if I obey them, my life will be better than the life I made listening to the other "voice" and going my own way. "

Days passed and I continued to read my Bible. I was resigned to believe God would never speak to me again. I felt I was not worthy of His presence anymore.

What I read in the Bible was meaningless. These were stories I'd heard all my life. I decided to just let the pages fall open anywhere and read whatever was there. To my surprise, this is what I read:

"Do not be afraid. You will not be ashamed or confused. You will not be put to shame and someday you will forget the shame of your youth. You won't even remember the reproach of not being a married woman. For I, the Lord God, am your husband. The Lord of All is my name. I am your Redeemer and the Holy One of Israel. I am the God of the whole Earth. I have called you, a woman forsaken and grieved in spirit. You are young and rejected. For a small moment in time I have forsaken you…but with great mercy I will draw you close to me. In a little wrath I hid my face from you for a time. But with everlasting kindness I will have mercy on you. I am the Lord, your Redeemer." (Isaiah 54:4-8)

Was this what I had begged for? Was this His way of "talking" to me? Did He truly mean that He would take me back in a good relationship?

I believed it was. I had heard people say that God "spoke" to them through the Bible, but this was the first time in many years I actually believed it.

It was as if God washed my soul with light, mercy and acceptance. I wept openly until all the hurt of the past seemed to stream out of my soul along with the tears.

I don't know how long I sat on the bathroom floor, Bible in my lap as I stroked that passage of scripture and seemed lifted beyond my earthly station into a higher place. Like a battered stray dog, I gladly accepted any crumb that fell from that heavenly table. I knew at that moment God had heard my cry...and I had heard His "voice."

Chapter 13: Settling Down

Days turned to weeks and weeks into another year as Jeff and I grew more stable in Dallas. Our social life revolved around our new church and bit by bit I gained confidence in myself.

I began to be more responsible for my actions. We learned to become part of the church by participating, not simply attending. We joined the choir.
Jeff was chosen to be on the church board and I was asked to teach a class of teens. Slowly, I got to know myself and our marriage was getting stronger.

It was in that church, we learned the joy of giving. Not only did we give a portion of our paycheck each week to help pay the expenses of keeping the building open and running, but we learned to give other things as well.

We decided the church needed a riding lawn mower. It was a big job in the summer, mowing all the grass around the building with push mowers, and it was all being done by volunteer labor. It wasn't that we had surplus money, but rather, we made the choice to sacrifice things we wanted for the good of the whole.

Imagine our displeasure, a week or two after we bought and delivered a new riding mower to the church, to see one of the kids (a son of a fellow who helped do the lawn work) racing around on the parking lot abusing the mower, driving it recklessly , kicking up rocks and dirt, like it was a toy!
We were still making payments on the machine. To see it being abused while his dad stood by watching was a real shock. We went home very discouraged. After praying about it though, we realized, our gift had been given to God…period! We learned a true gift has no strings attached. After it leaves our hands, it's not our responsibility to see that it gets used as we think it should.

Whoever uses what we gave to God is responsible to Him…not us. Knowing that, helped us release our emotion and trust God's control of anything we gave Him.
I continued soaking myself in the scripture. It was as if I'd never heard it; like passages were personal

letters written just for me. I learned to talk to God all day. I found He had a great sense of humor and loved to laugh. I learned more about his nature during those few years we lived in Dallas than I'd known all the years I'd been exposed to church. I was learning to live my life by believing the Bible was true and simply acting as if it were, even when I had doubts.

Chapter 14: Our First House

A year after we moved into the little rent house, our landlord decided to sell it. We were forced to find another rental or buy the house we occupied. Jeff's parents had never owned a house, so it was very disconcerting for him to decide to buy instead of rent.

On the other hand, my family had owned most of the houses we lived in, so I persuaded him to take a chance by committing to buy. I think he was concerned about losing his income. The aircraft industry paid well when it had contracts, but what would we do if he was laid off again?

Long-term financial obligation was unfamiliar to him. The only time he ever borrowed money was $1,400 for a used truck, and we were still making payments on it. He didn't want to be overextended, borrowing money to buy the house.

When pushed to make a decision of moving or staying with a mortgage over our head, he finally chose the latter.

As a young family, this gave us experience of negotiating a home loan.
He grumbled the whole time he filled out forms that revealed all our financial information. As a very private person, he thought the bank asked for too much information.

Now I chuckle about our naivety after we bought several homes sequentially to this one and a small farm where we live today in our retirement.

Despite the fears, we bought our first house. We signed the papers and then owned the same house we had rented. The payments dropped from $85 per month to $83 per month…but there was a pride we felt in the little house that had become ours on a thirty- year loan for $7,500.

We were both growing into adults instead of the insecure young teens we were when we married. The maturity was good, but it required a lot of change in both of us…and a lot of faith.

Chapter 15: Another Move

Money was tight, so Jeff decided home construction business was something he would like to do...and the timing was perfect. The building glut of the late 60's was just beginning. He hated the unexpected lay-offs at the airplane factory and thought he could develop another career. So, he found extra work at a door manufacturing company nearby for more experience and some more money.

Gaining a little experience painting our house, he started painting rent houses for our former landlord, Ken. This was in addition to his regular job and his part-time job.

One day he heard news of a contractor who needed workers to help re-do destroyed HUD homes. The pay was better than the door factory, so he quit there and worked extra hours each day for the building contractor. It was steady pay for another 20 hours of work per week.

All this time, he continued painting houses on the

weekends. He began contracting jobs in addition to the work Ken provided. He charged $250 per house if the customer provided the paint.

Then, Dallas County passed a court order to bus students from one area to another. It was forced integration, and I think both races felt the same way. We didn't want it. It was imposed on us.

Although we lived only a block away from the grade school Adam would attend in the fall, we were informed he would be bused to another school located on the other side of the freeway. He was only six years old. We knew we weren't the only parents concerned about those changes…so, like many others in our neighborhood, we considered relocating. We could place Adam in private school and stay where we were, which would stretch our budget to tearing limits, or relocate outside Dallas County.

At Jeff's reluctance, I began another house search with his strict requirements, such as…a hip roof, copper wiring, 2"x 6" rafters and 16" spacing on wall studs. Many of the builders were cutting costs then by not using *any* of these features! Although his salary had gradually increased over the years, the payments could not exceed $200 per month.

I searched outside Dallas County in my little $450-1956-two-toned Chevy Jeff bought to meet my needs. I had to consider the cost of Jeff's commute to work in Grand Prairie. He was accustomed to driving 70 miles per day. This was in 1971 when gasoline prices kept rising.

I looked at several houses and discovered many of the builders used aluminum wiring, no hip roofs, and fewer wall studs than Jeff required. Usually the houses were separated only by a few feet apart on very small lots.

Each time I persuaded Jeff to go look at a house, he found so much wrong with it, I scratched it off the list and started again.

I began praying God would help me find the right house.

One Friday I drove to Midlothian, a tiny town south of Dallas, and stopped at Sewell Realty on the main street. I told the older lady our requirements. She shuffled through her desk papers, then stood up and removed her glasses attached to a long gold chain, and let them dangle around her neck.

Then Mrs. Sewell said, "Sweetheart, I'm sure I can find something suitable on our list. Why don't we get in my car and I'll show you some of our properties?"

So we loaded into her Cadillac and drove around Midlothian looking at new homes that were more than $400 per month. They were beautiful and well built…but not what we could afford.

After I convinced her that we must have something less expensive, she finally remembered a little house that had been on the market for awhile. It had contracted several times, but none of the customers qualified for a loan. It was recently listed again.

We drove down a quiet street on the edge of town and parked in front of a little brick house with a hip roof.

"I'm sure this one will be perfect for you," she said. "It was built by one of the best builders in town. His dad built houses for years and Gary Hayes learned the trade from his dad. This is Gary's first speculative build, but I know it is a good house. He has built custom homes with his dad since he was a kid."

When she opened the door, the smell was still new. It was about 1,200 square feet with a formal living room, kitchen/dining area, den with sliding glass patio doors, three bedrooms, two full baths, a laundry area, and an enclosed garage. The back yard was small, but the front yard was deep and had a large tree…AND…it was the right price. Only $22,000!

"Does this house have copper wiring?" I asked. "How far apart are the wall studs?"

Mrs. Sewell wrinkled her forehead and told me "You know…I don't know the answer to those questions, but I can give you the builder's phone number and you can ask him."

It was getting late in the day and I needed to get home to cook Jeff's supper. I really wanted him to see the house that day before daylight faded. I was trying not to be too excited and said, "Thank you for showing me this house, Mrs. Sewell. I think it is just what we are looking for, but my husband will have to see the house too. Could I make an appointment for this weekend to view it again?"

To my surprise, she twisted the house key off her key ring and handed it to me.

"Here, honey, take this with you. Y'all come whenever you want. You can bring the key back to me when you're finished with it. Now let's go back to the office and get that phone number for you."

"Are you sure you want to leave the key with me? I mean, I may not get Jeff to come before your office closes today. I noticed you are not open on the weekends."

She chuckled and said, "Sweetie…you just keep the key and bring it back Monday. Your husband needs to see the house too and he'll probably want to meet Gary. Call him when you get home and he'll answer all your questions."

I was astonished at the instant trust she had in me. It was a foreshadowing of the warmth we would find in that little bedroom community.

After we finished supper, during which I rattled like a magpie about finding the little house with all its wonderful features, I finally convinced Jeff to look at the house in Midlothian. He was tired, so it took some "cheerleading" to convince him this house wasn't like all the others he'd viewed.

He rolled his eyes when I said "Please, honey. She gave me the key and I know you'll be impressed. It has a hip roof and everything and it's only $22,000!

He was very skeptical, but we made the twenty-minute drive and arrived slightly before sunset.

I was dancing on a tight wire all the time Jeff wandered through the house opening closets, checking the plumbing, tapping on the walls to find the studs. He even crawled up into the attic to see the wiring. It was copper!

He couldn't believe the price for the quality. He definitely wanted to talk to the builder.

Gary Hayes met us at the house the next afternoon as soon as Jeff got off work. He was a quiet man with a calm demeanor. He and Jeff discussed the house in depth.

"It's a good house." Gary said. "I don't understand why it hasn't sold already. It's been on the market for almost a year. There've been three contracts, but nobody qualified for the loan." Ours would be the fourth.

I daydreamed about the possibility of our getting the new house. It had avocado- colored kitchen appliances. The sink was matching color with a garbage disposal! Flocked wallpaper in the dining area made it look so modern.
The laundry room was located inside the house

instead of out in the garage. It was so beautiful I mentally placed our furniture in each room.

Some people think things happen by coincidence...but I was beginning to believe that things happen by orchestration. *Had God led me to Midlothian and kept that little house available just for us?* When we qualified for the loan, I believed that was the case.

We decided not to sell the little house in Dallas but use it as rental property for additional income.

We relocated in Midlothian, Texas, in June, 1972. The little bedroom community south of Dallas seemed untouched by the big city atmosphere.
I think that's one reason Jeff agreed to move.

The town had a much slower pace than Dallas. One of the grocery stores was so old fashioned it still loaded purchases in cardboard boxes instead of brown bags. There was only one four-way stop in the whole town. The local newspaper was as thin as a quarter and cost the same. We loved it!
Schools weren't crowded and were loaded with

dedicated teachers that moved there for the same reasons we did...to have a better quality life in the country.

A local dairy allowed us to buy whole, unprocessed milk from them if we brought our empty milk cartons for them to fill. I made home churned butter from the cream that lay on top of the milk.

Confident parents let their children ride bikes in the neighborhood and play at the neighbor's houses without worry. Families visited each other and had ice cream parties in the summertime. Downtown streets were closed for every Fourth of July parade. The highlight of each week was the local football games in the fall. We felt we had stepped back in time.

I got a job as a salesclerk at a sporting goods store in Dallas to help pay bills. Jeff found that our renters were not always dependable and he said my working would only be temporary.

One of the teens in my Sunday class at church in

Dallas was glad when she got the job of babysitting Adam for me while I was at work till he started first grade in September.

At first, everything was perfect. I didn't have to be at work till nine o'clock in the morning…so I had time to pre-cook supper and take Adam to the sitter's. Jeff picked him up after he got off work at 4 pm and I was home by 6:00 pm.

Jeff continued working his full-time job, but because I worked, he could quit his part-time job. However, he still painted houses. Before he finished painting one house, another was contracted. He had several jobs on the waiting list.

My life was so busy then. I didn't think we could add any more activity anywhere, but God had a different plan. I got pregnant!

Chapter 16: Pregnant Again

Jeff and I didn't think we could have more children. I tried to get pregnant when Adam was two years old when we still lived in Dallas, but I had female problems. After three surgeries, my gynecologist told me not to worry about it. Just enjoy unprotected sex. If I got pregnant, it was meant to be.

So, we did for six years! After that long a time, getting pregnant was a total surprise for both of us…but the timing seemed so wrong. We didn't know how we could provide for another child.

During my pregnancy, I had been told I could work until my fifth month of pregnancy. Then, I would be laid off without pay. Of course, I could come back to work after the birth. At that time, I modeled high-dollar ladies' wear on Saturdays as part of the sales job, and I couldn't do that in maternity clothes. I began to pray that God would somehow show us a way we could afford my lay-off.

Secretly, I longed to stay home with the new baby, as

I had with Adam, until the child was old enough to start school, but I couldn't see any way. I talked to Jeff about not going back to work after my pregnancy leave.

"Honey, I can't see any way you can quit your job unless you help me paint more houses. If we can get enough painting jobs to pay the bills, then you could stay home with the baby."

So, during the months I was off work, I helped Jeff paint houses. All the while, I prayed for a financial miracle to allow me to stay home after the baby was born.

One hot Saturday in July, we were painting a house. I tucked in a cooler of sandwiches and drinks, brought along toys to occupy Adam, and wore my not-so-feminine work clothes.

About 2:00 pm, the temperature had risen past one-hundred degrees. The lady of the house came out on the porch and saw me standing on a ladder painting trim, my belly as big as a watermelon. She must have pitied me.

Offering Adam and me a glass of iced water she said, "Honey, you shouldn't be up on that ladder in this heat in your condition. Why don't you come inside where it's cool?"

I smiled, my face flushed with heat. Between swigs I said "Oh, no, ma'am. It's okay. I do this all the time. Thanks for your concern though." I was miserable, but we needed the money more than I needed my comfort.

I look back now and shake my head at my determination to stay home with the baby. It made me pray all the more for that miracle to happen.
I realized how very much God loved us and provided for us. He gave our family good health and Jeff's love for us enabled him to give of himself to afford the best he could offer. I was so blessed. Each afternoon he rushed home from his job, gulped down his supper and we were ready to go paint a house.

I used a paint roller to apply the paint the customer

bought, and Jeff followed behind with a brush (a technique he discovered watching painters on the remodeling job). Adam was so well behaved, he entertained himself nearby and in no time, we had jobs lined up one after another. We worked for half the rate of union painters and were out nothing but our gasoline and time.

We didn't mind hard work. We were young and eager to have all the conveniences of other young families. The pace was fierce, but the money came in.

Our church helped with a huge baby shower. We didn't have to buy anything but baby food the first year! I knew God had planned this baby.
We still tithed our money and God never let us miss a payment on any of our obligations.

 I believed Philippians 4:19..."But my God shall supply all your need according to his riches in glory by Christ Jesus." Another scripture said, "Bring a tenth of what you make into my storehouse, so that there may be food in my house. Test me this day and see if I will not throw the floodgates of heaven open and pour so much blessing on you there will not be enough room for it." (Malachi 3:10)   Indeed, He did.

Chapter 17: Leaving Our Church Family

During those first years in Midlothian, we were still driving to our Dallas church. A young woman who lived close to us, and also went to our church, invited me to an all-denominational Bible study. It was led by a lady of a different denomination than ours. My friend convinced me I could learn a lot more in a study that included women of all doctrines and ages. They met once a week for study and pot-luck lunch. I'd never attended any Bible study outside my Mom's denomination. *What would it be like to mix my beliefs with others who might not have the same opinion?* It was a new concept. Hesitantly, I agreed to go with her at least once and check it out. Prideful, I felt I probably knew more Bible than most of them anyway.

We arrived at a lovely home in a small addition outside Lancaster, Texas. There were at least fifteen women there. Most were older than me, but all had children either there in the playroom, or at school. I listened to their chatter and laughter and longed to be accepted. Nisha slept in her baby tender beside my chair as I listened attentively to the leader. She explained the method of study.

"For those new visitors among us, we welcome you. No matter what your church affiliation or level of spiritual maturity, we want you to help teach this class. My format is simply this: I assign a portion of scripture each week for us to study. Each of us will write a paraphrase of that scripture.
You may use only seven words per verse to complete your assignment. As you distill your thoughts, keep in mind that you will ask yourself two questions:
What did I learn from this portion of God's word and how will I put it into practice in my life?
When you return to class the next week, we will each share what God has taught us about His standards and what He has taught us about ourselves."

That day, I listened closely to each woman as she read her paraphrase and discussed her revelations. There was warmth in the class that enveloped me…but there was also an incredible honesty among them. They were not ashamed to admit their faults to each other and shared incidences of their failings and successes. Nobody in the group seemed judgmental.

They accepted the fact that they didn't meet all the standards, yet encouraged each other to practice doing every day the principles they learned until it became habit in their lives. It was a "hands-on" learning method...a different type of "group therapy".

The ladies Bible study I attended opened up a new world to me. I never considered that God wanted to teach me His word so thoroughly. I always thought the Bible needed to be interpreted by someone in authority...someone "called to preach the Gospel". I never knew that I could have my own opinion of what the scriptures meant. Being in that class brought a new excitement to my study time. It wasn't long before I couldn't wait each morning to grab my Bible and have private time with the Lord, letting Him teach me what He wanted me to know.

I learned to cross-reference scriptures I didn't understand. I bought a Bible Concordance, a topical Bible, and other study tools I never knew existed. Gradually, I understood the reasons behind all those rules I'd hated. The rules were only a recipe for a happy life. I could follow them or not. It had always been my choice. God was, indeed, renewing my mind.

We kept trying to be involved with our church in Dallas, but the drive and distance began draining us. We sang in the choir, I taught a class every Sunday, Jeff served on the church board, in short, we were working so hard during the week AND on Sundays we experienced "burn out".

After praying about it, I felt our sphere of influence should be where we were now living, in Midlothian. However, I was battling leaving the ones in my Sunday class God had entrusted to me. I felt no one else would care like I did.

A week later I stopped by our church in Dallas. It was with mixed feelings I sat in the parking lot reliving the years God had given us in this loving environment. I recalled the lessons we had learned and the friends who loved us just as we were. Some of them are lifelong friends today.
Then I saw Pastor Williams walking across the parking lot to my car. After we talked for a few

minutes I approached him with the news that we would be finding a new church in Midlothian. His reaction was not what I expected. His voice choked with tears as he begged us not to leave his church. "You are making a terrible mistake, Ann. If you leave your friends, those who care about you, there's a risk you will lose all you've gained. You just can't afford to do that."

Robert had counseled us like a parent through some rough trials. I felt he was the kind of dad I never had. His warning shocked me and made me doubt my decision.

He continued. "I'm afraid you are taking a step in the wrong direction. You will never find a church that meets your needs the way this one does."

Were we taking the wrong step to find a church in our town in which to serve? I told him I'd pray about it again…but I felt certain that was what God wanted us to do. I told him I'd do whatever God led me to do. Sometimes a believer just has to trust the "voice" he heard was God's. I didn't want to be wrong about the voices in my head again. Yet, I had been guided by this man's wisdom for several years and trusted his voice, too.

Again, I had to trust my faith that God would keep us in His care no matter what. He would have to lead us instead of our pastor in Dallas.

We tried several churches in our town, but none seemed to meet our heart's cry until a friend of mine in the lady's Bible study told me about a new little church that was meeting in a house on the northwest side of Midlothian.

We visited the next Wednesday night and found a spirit of love and fellowship we knew was right. The young pastor was still in training at Dallas Theological Seminary but had a great understanding of the scriptures. He could explain things clearly and had a heart full of love and compassion for people. We later signed the charter as two of the first seventy-five members of a church that grew to be the largest church in Midlothian. Dave Wyrtzen is their Pastor Emeritus to this day.

Chapter 18: God Reveals Himself

God answered my prayer for a miracle in June of 1974. After Jeff earned his first big promotion at the airplane factory, I was able to stay home with our daughter, Nisha, who was born in the fall. We were finally able to quit painting houses.

It was during that time I wrestled with the idea that God looks at his followers as sheep. In several scriptures, he mentioned that his sheep knew his voice (John 10: 3-4).

I told God I really didn't know the difference between His voice and Satan's voice. They sounded the same in my head. It all was just thoughts that came into my mind. The voice I heard sounded like my own, but the thoughts seemed to come from beyond…out of nowhere. I began asking God to teach me to hear the difference, so that I would not be deceived again. It was then God began teaching me in a very visual way to recognize His voice.

One morning, about 2:00 am, I dreamed I was in a

dark loft overlooking a large room far below. The room was brightly lit and filled with people having a fun time. Laughing children chased each other. Music played, and the murmur of voices hummed in the background. There was a clatter of dishes and the savory smell of food being prepared. I longed to be down there with them, but could see no way out of the loft.

I turned slightly and was disgusted by the filth I saw in my surroundings. There was no light in the room except what filtered up from the room below. Old newspapers, dirty rags and trash lay stacked around. Cobwebs filled each corner, and dirt was caked on the bare wooden floor. It was as if the room had been neglected for years and was dying for want of use.

As I turned further around, I was startled by what I saw. An old man was sitting on the floor with his back against the wall. His grey, tufted hair was unkempt and his clothes were tattered as if he, too, had been locked in that room for years. He smiled at me as our eyes met.

In a rather nonchalant way, he spoke to me about the condition of the loft.

"Looks pretty nasty doesn't it? It's been this way a long time. I know you want to join the folks below, but the only way you can get out of here is to clean up this mess first."

"But that's impossible," I said. "I have nothing to clean it with…no broom, no mop, no soap. This room is going to take a LOT of work. I don't even know where to start!"

He chuckled. "Oh, I'll help you with it. Go ahead. I won't do the work for you, but I can tell you what to do. Why not start by picking up all the trash and stacking it together, so you can get rid of it?"

"Are you sure that's all I have to do to get out of here…just clean up this nasty room?"

"That's it." he said with a shrug and a smile. Mentally, I wondered why he never wanted to get out of that ugly loft enough to clean the room himself!

Skeptically, I began to pick up the trash and organize it. I hadn't been busy long when I lifted a large pile of papers and was frightened as a rat the size of a small dog jumped from under the paper, raised up on his hind legs and hissed at me, fangs bared. His teeth were at least four inches long!

Startled, I jumped back out of its way, almost stumbling in a heap, trying to get away from it.

"Hey", I yelled at the old man…"that thing almost bit me! I'm not cleaning anything with that rat in here!"

"Oh, he won't hurt you. He's been here for years. He knows if you clean this room, he won't have anywhere to live. He'll have to go elsewhere. He's just trying to scare you, so you won't clean up the room." Just let him know you aren't afraid of him. Work around him. In a little bit, he'll stay out of your way."

With that bit of advice, I woke up.

With my eyes wide open, I wondered what the dream meant. Then, God spoke to me.

"Ann, you have been keeping so much filth and sin in your heart for years that it has completely filled your being. I have a plan for your life but to become the person you really want to be you'll have to start rearranging your life. I'll help you do this through my Word, but you must practice what you learn for it to work. Satan will try to discourage you with fear, but just keep practicing. Little by little your attitudes and actions will become changed into a beautiful new person, a new you. You are now a part of my kingdom here on earth, and you will learn to live in that kingdom. In the process, you will find great joy, a settling new peace, and plenty of wonderful things in your life. You will truly have a new heart."

I pondered what He said and made a new commitment to obey His voice, His Word, with all my being.
It was only a few days after that revelation that I began to learn how to change.

I was reading my Bible and in Proverbs 3:5 I found that new way of living. It said "Trust in the Lord with ALL your heart. Don't lean on what you feel is right, but acknowledge God in ALL your doings and let Him direct your actions." *What exactly did that mean for me?*

I took those words literally and began asking God's direction for every moment of the day. It may seem simple and rather unnecessary for some of you to believe that I took that scripture literally, but it totally changed my life. For a period of several weeks, I asked the Lord's direction for everything I did every moment of the day.

When I got up in the morning and started to dress, I would ask, "Okay, Lord…what do you want me to wear?" Sometimes He would say, "Put on your work clothes, Ann. We've got a lot to do today." Then He'd proceed to tell me each chore to do next. At first, I really didn't want to do all He said, like scrubbing toilets until they gleamed, cleaning out the kitchen cabinets, or pulling the weeds in my flower beds. However, through my obedience I will share with you story after story the lessons He taught me about his nature while I obeyed. We had such wonderful fellowship. I was beginning to know the personality of

God himself and His love for me through my obedience. He was, indeed, teaching me to know His voice and His personality.

Some days, I would go into my closet and, surprisingly, He would tell me to dress to go out. I would have NO idea when or where we would be going, but shortly I would be on an adventure I hadn't imagined for that day.

He altered recipes for me and made them tastier. He told me how to repair things I had no expertise in doing. He told me which line to get into at the bank drive-through to save time. All I had to do was listen closely to Him, and he would tell me exactly what to do, just like his scripture said.

On one of these days I was instructed to dress nicely for the day. I hesitated because it was raining, not drops, but buckets! We were under a flash flood watch and I really didn't think it was wise to drive anywhere at the time. Maybe the Lord would wait until the rain stopped to tell me why I had to dress that way.

But He didn't. I had fed, bathed and dressed Nisha when He said it was time to go.

"Go where, Lord?" I asked.

"We are going to pick up Plaster of Paris for Vacation Bible School this morning." I was the Craft Director for the event at our church and knew I would need the plaster soon.

"But, Lord, in case you haven't noticed, it is raining BIG time right now. I really don't think it's a safe time to be out, especially with my baby."

He quietly reminded me of a scripture I had just memorized. "When you pass through the waters, I will be with you; and the rivers will not overflow you; when you walk through the fire, you will not be burned, neither will the flame touch you" (Isaiah 43:2).

Did I believe that? Yes, I did...sort of. I think God wanted to give me proof after I thought I believed Him. Moments later, I had the baby loaded and we took off. It wasn't that I was totally without fear, but I had learned in days previous to trust His voice. He never told me anything that contradicted the written Word. It was always "in line" with the scriptures and their meanings. I learned that simple obedience was what He wanted. He would keep me safe, but it was imperative that I learn His nature through the scriptures and obedience to Him. Then, I could discern His voice. It's odd that the other "voice" I'd heard had brought so much pain in my life, but God's voice, in alliance with His Word, always brought new insight and joy.

I headed to the nearest paint store in a town nearby. On the way, I stopped behind a car that had been stalled in the road. I couldn't get around it. The rain was so fierce, coming down in blustery sheets, I couldn't see to pass. I sat there a minute thinking at anytime the lady behind the wheel of the car would get it started. I saw vaguely the back seat was loaded with kids. Then, the Lord spoke.

"If you see a person in need...meet that need" (James 2:15).

"But, Lord…SHE needs a tow truck…not me!" I sat behind the wheel thinking about her need. She had a carload of kids she couldn't leave in the middle of the road and a car that would not start because the battery had probably been overtaxed by her over-cranking the car. I knew that because I'd done it a few times myself. This was before the days of cell phones so how was she going to get help?

Reluctantly, I grabbed my umbrella, jumped out of my car and tapped on her window. Startled and wild-eyed, she opened it slightly and listened.
"You need a tow truck," I yelled, above the roar of the rain. "I'll drive to the next station and see if I can get help for you. I'll be back in a few minutes." She nodded her head…mind you…no "thank you" went with that nod.

I silently grumbled and told the Lord to take note of my obedience this time.
I deserved at least half a gold star for this one.

I drove to the nearest station and told the owner the lady's plight. He cast a glance upward and said,

"Lady, I will go help her as soon as this rain lets up but not right now." I thanked him (for nothing) and drove to the next station.

The attendant there told me, "We don't have a tow truck, ma'am. Otherwise, I'd be happy to help. There's a station two blocks down that has the equipment. I quickly thanked him and headed to the next station.

I saw the tow truck parked outside and felt a rush of excitement that my wild-goose chase had ended. The man inside the station promised me he'd go check on her.

FINALLY! I thanked the fellow, crawled back in my car soaking wet, and returned to the stalled car to tell her help was on the way. I upped the half- star to a whole one as I reminded the Lord how obedient I was being.

When I rounded the corner and glanced down the street where she had been, I was shocked. The car was gone! She had started the dumb thing and left!

All my effort for NOTHING!

"Now, what was THAT all about, God! I did exactly what you told me and for WHAT?!"

I could see absolutely NO purpose in all that inconvenience and all of it for NOTHING. I was puffing with indignation, my clothes soaked and my wet hair molded to my head.

He paused for a moment, and then He spoke. "Ann, I have lots of people that call themselves by my name, but few that will do the things I ask of them. For instance, if I ask them to meet a need, some will look at their circumstances and say, "It's not a convenient time to do this now, Lord. I'll do it later." Or, another will say, "I don't have the ability to do that. Ask somebody else." Or sometimes, I will have someone tell me "yes," but they don't obey immediately. When they finally do...the opportunity is gone. That's why it is important for you to obey the moment I prompt you.

I sat there, rain pattering on the windshield, thanking God for giving me such a clear, visual lesson...one I'd never forget. I vowed not to complain again whenever He asked me to do something that was inconvenient or taxing. How soon I would forget my vow. I drove on to the paint store, still mulling the events in my mind.

After purchasing the plaster and running back to my car, I shifted into gear and started out of the parking lot. I felt good about obeying the Lord, despite the circumstances and was rewarding myself with a spiritual "pat on the back" when He said, "Turn left, Ann."

'Turn, left? But Lord to go back home, I have to turn right."

Silence. I had heard Him correctly.

Although I didn't understand, I turned left and started out of town in a direction I'd never been before. Residential areas and places of business gradually melted away and soon I was on a lonely road miles from home. Like a cracked rock with water seeping through it, my faith began to weaken.

"Where are we going, Lord? Did I hear you correctly?" No answer.

I glanced at the gas gauge and saw that it registered only a "click" above the empty zone. *Oh, dear. Now I'm almost out of gas!*

"God, do you HEAR me? I'm out of gas and there's not a gas station anywhere that I can see!"

Silence.

I continued down the road, mustering the courage to obey even though circumstances looked bleak. It got worse.

The road took a bend and faded into a less-traveled course. Weeds grew tall along the pock-marked lane. I was forced to turn sharply left and saw that the road went under an old concrete railroad trestle. Broken beer bottles and trash littered the area. Fear began to take over.
This is stupid! You're going into an area that doesn't look a bit safe. You're out of gas AND you're taking

your baby with you! Are you SURE you heard God's voice?

I glanced at the gas gauge and saw it sitting in the red zone. I began to pray that God would give me some sign that I was truly doing what He wanted. I needed to know I was not being misled by my own imagination…or the wrong "voice."

The road straightened and my eyes began searching for anything familiar.
To the right of the road, along an old barbed-wire fence, peeping through weeds as tall as cornstalks was a faded sign. Not just one sign, but several.

They read: "This will never
　　　　　　Come to pass
　　　　　A backseat driver
　　　　　Out of gas."
　　　　　Burma Shave

So does that mean I won't run out of gas, even though the gas gauge was on EMPTY? Was that my answer from God?

I kept on driving. The road improved and I found myself approaching a neighborhood lined with run-down rental houses. Each yard was cluttered: old cars and trucks (some without tires), children's toys, a rusted old washing machine. It wasn't any more encouraging than the forsaken area I'd just come through…but at least, I thought, there should be a gas station near. Then God spoke again.

"Stop at the third house on your left. Go to the door and say to whoever answers the door, "God loves you, and so do I."

Oh, no, Lord! Surely I didn't hear you correctly. I don't know anybody in this neighborhood! What will happen if some drunk man answers the door and has crazy ideas when I say that?!"

I argued a few moments longer, but hearing no answer, reluctantly pulled into the driveway and parked. I left the car running and Nisha inside. I wanted to make a quick get-away after I delivered the message.
The rain had almost stopped. There was a thick mist

still in the air as I climbed out of the car. I approached the front door with its outer screen door hanging by one hinge. There was no doorbell, so I knocked. My heart was pounding in my throat.

A long pause gave relief. I assumed no one was there.

Turning to leave, I quipped, "I get it, Lord. This was just a test to see if I'd obey, right? Very funny!" Then, the door opened.

To my great surprise as I turned, I saw a young woman at the door, her belly swelled with pregnancy. I knew her!

Jackie was a teen when I first met her. I had taken my Sunday class canvassing local apartments near our church in Dallas. She was standing in the parking lot, baby on her hip and two small children with her. She had been left in charge of the family while her mom, who birthed each child by a different man, was at work. Jackie was old for her age. She longed to have a little freedom and anybody to care. We filled the bill. She began coming to church and found new friends and salvation there. Apparently, a lot had happened in her life since then.

She was as surprised to see me as I was to see her. She blinked through swollen eyes and stood there in the doorway, barefoot and sniffling, as I delivered the message. She ducked her head and then said something remarkable.

"You're not going to believe this, Ann. I just prayed this morning that IF God was real, He would show me before the hour was gone or else I was going to kill myself and the baby."

I glanced over her shoulder and saw the pistol lying on the couch behind her. My heart bled for her brokenness. In a few short years, her joy had turned into misery. I unloaded Nisha from the car, sat on the couch with her and listened to her story. She told me she had met a guy who said he loved her. Shortly after, she lost interest in church and quit coming. About a year ago, she'd moved in with him and soon after, had gotten pregnant. Evidence of his lack of care for her was parked in her kitchen...a huge motorcycle, caked with mud and grease. Dishes were piled in the sink and a large, wet German shepherd dog lay in the doorway. She was overwhelmed.

I let her talk and then encouraged her to leave the guy. I advised, "Go to some church nearby and get help. Tell the pastor your story, and I will pray that the church will be a loving one that will put actions to their claim of being Christians (like Christ) and help you become independent." She had no phone to keep in touch with me, so I gave her my phone number and told her to call me from the church where she might get help. If not, I would come back and help her move myself. I held her hand and prayed that God would give her the courage to leave this man. She promised me she would and said she would let me know the outcome.

I don't know what happened to Jackie after that. I never got a phone call and when I drove back a few days later to check on her, the house was vacant. I had to leave her in God's hands. I was learning to trust He would take care of those I loved, even those who were weak in faith.

As I backed out of Jackie's driveway that morning, I praised God that He allowed me to minister for Him that morning. *What if I had not obeyed?*

"Oh, Lord...please supply me strength to obey you at all times," I prayed. "Remind me of the lessons you have taught me today. Don't let me forget the importance of instant obedience." I sobbed for Jackie and the sadness in her life. I knew God could change her life, just as he was changing mine. I wondered how many more "Jackie's" were out in the world, lost and hopeless.

I had to find a gas station...quickly! A few blocks closer to town, I pulled into the first station in sight and pumped my last three dollars into the tank.

At least the rain had stopped, and I was confident of my way home from the little town of Lancaster, Texas. Nisha was beginning to get fussy. She had finished her bottle of juice and was working on a bottle of water, but she had a healthy appetite, and I hadn't brought any baby food. It was almost lunchtime, and she was getting hungry. She was down to her last clean diaper, too. I never dreamed I would be gone so long.

I steered the car toward home when I heard the "voice" again.

"Ann, I want you to go to Betty's house before going home."

Betty was a friend from our church in Dallas who lived in Lancaster. She loved to laugh and share stories with me, but she had a habit of conversing "one-way", meaning I listened and she talked...and talked...and talked. I knew if I obeyed the Lord, I would be tied up at least another hour before I could feed Nisha. I spent my last dime on gas and my baby could get really ugly if she wasn't fed on time.

However, considering the morning's "miracles," I trusted the Lord had something additionally special for me. At that moment, Nisha was content with only water. I drove straight to Betty's house.

When I arrived, I rang the doorbell but nobody came to the door. Had I misunderstood? I rang the bell again and again…still nothing. Betty was not at home.

I was puzzled. "Lord, did I hear you correctly? Didn't you say "Go to Betty's house?"

"Yes, I did, Ann, but I didn't tell you she wouldn't be at home. Now you must go next door to her neighbor's house."

"But, Lord, I scarcely know her! I only met her a few months ago when she came with Betty to church. What do I say when she comes to the door?"

He was through talking.

I moved the car into her driveway and loaded my beginning-to-be-irritable baby in my arms.

As I pushed the doorbell, I was thinking how silly this was. God knew I had a hungry baby and no food. I had no money and my pantry was at least 30 minutes away. How was He going to solve this one?

"Well, hello, Ann!" the neighbor said as she opened the storm door. "Come in here and I'll make some coffee." She held open the door as she continued.

"I was so bored and lonely this morning. I had surgery a couple of weeks ago and I can't drive yet. I've watched all the TV I can stand. You are just what I need!"

"I really can't stay long," I apologized and said, "I came to see Betty but she wasn't home and….."

"Oh, I'm sooo glad!" she interrupted, "I think Betty is gone for the day. Here, let me help you." She rattled on and on as she was shifting Nisha into her arms while Nisha let out a howl and arched her little back as if to say, "This is NOT what I want! I told you I wanted food…not cuddling!"

She cooed to Nisha and jostled her around, trying to make her comfortable.

I explained. "I've been gone from home too long, and I don't have any baby food with me. I expected to be home by now. I'm sorry I can't stay and visit long. It's time for Nisha's lunch and nap."

By this time, Nisha was in full hunger mode, flailing her arms, kicking and screaming, not a pleasant experience for a mom introducing her little "bundle of joy" for the first time.

I took my baby from her arms and began gathering my things as I said, "I'm so sorry I can't stay. I really must get home and feed this child."

Like a fairy godmother, an enlightened expression spread over her face. She quickly led me into her kitchen, yanked open the pantry door and displayed shelves full of baby food.
"Voila!" she exclaimed, bending like a Master of Ceremonies with arms leading my eyes toward the pantry contents. "I had stomach surgery and have to eat baby food for a month. What would she like to eat? Let's see…carrots, peas, chicken, fruit…or a little of all?"

My mouth dropped open. Silently I breathed a prayer of thanks that God had not forgotten my needs as he used me to meet other's needs. What a great God I served!

We sat and chatted over coffee as I fed Nisha a fine lunch. Contented, she nestled in my arms and fell asleep after a bottle of milk. I was able to stay and visit with Betty's neighbor for a while. She was really lonely and seemed elated to have some company.

All the while we talked, I was overwhelmed by the idea my God knew everyone's needs and could meet them all if only his followers would be obedient to His commands. His "rules" began to make sense.
You can't imagine the sense of awe I felt the remainder of the day. I could hardly wait until Jeff came home to tell him about my day. He must have felt I was ready for the "funny farm" again when he heard everything. It was all too fantastic, too unbelievable, and yet...it was all true. I was living in a world that wasn't imaginary...but it was beyond my wildest dreams.

Chapter 19: The Tupperware Story

Days followed, and with them new lessons learned. One of my favorite visuals from God was the "Tupperware" lesson.

It was springtime. All the windows were open and I was busy as a bird cleaning her nest. My head was thrust deep into the bottom cabinets of the kitchen. I was unloading the entire contents, placing them around me on the floor so that I could scrub the shelves and install new shelf paper when God spoke.

"What do you see around you, Ann?"

"Well, I see a bunch of dishes, bowls, cookware..."

"No," he said. "Look closer, Ann, and tell me what you really see?"

It was then I realized He had some kind of visual lesson going here.
"I see my good china. It's so beautiful. Thank you for it. Every time I dig it out of the back of the cabinet, I

enjoy looking at it. Its beauty gives me a lot of pleasure."

"But, how often do you use it?" He asked.

"Not very often, Lord, only on rare occasions. I'm afraid it will get chipped or broken."

"Okay," he said. "What else do you see?"

I looked around at the stuff piled about me. Most of it was just a hodge-podge of mixing bowls, Cool Whip tubs, and "odds and ends."

"Which of all of these is your favorite piece?" the Lord asked.

I picked up my favorite Tupperware bowl and looked at it closely. It was stained. It had deep scratches in the bottom from mixing things. It even had part of the side melted because I sat it too close to the burner one day. The lid was cracked. I don't know why I kept it except I used it almost every day.

Gently the Lord spoke. "Ann, I want you to be a Tupperware bowl.

"A Tupperware bowl? Whatever do you mean?"

He continued, "I have lots of children who are beautiful, like your china, pristine...perfect. They look great on the surface, but they can't be used.
They are afraid they will get chipped or broken."

He continued, "I want you to be a Tupperware bowl. You will be scratched and stained. Melted and cracked...but you know what? I will use you every day."

As I processed the magnitude of what He'd said, I wept with joy at how loved God made me feel. All the hurt and bitterness, the pain I'd been through was for a reason...and would continue to be so. He made me feel so precious, so special. Then, he reminded me of a scripture that fit hand-in-glove with the visual lesson.

I Peter 1: 6-7 "You can now rejoice a lot, even if for a

time you suffer greatly in many ways. Because the trials that test your faith are more precious than earthly gold. Even if you are tested with fire…you can be found faithful (useful) to God which brings praise, honor and glory to Christ Jesus."

Chapter 20: Knowing Fear

I was so immersed in the presence of God that even though I knew I lived in a physical world, it seemed I was observing it in a different way. I was in the world, yet not a part of it. That's tough to explain, but I believe any Christian who has walked close to God has known what I felt.

There are scriptures that speak about being in this world…but not being a part of this world. In a prayer just before His crucifixion Jesus said to God, the heavenly Father, (John 17:14-17) "I have given my disciples your truth: the world now hates them because they are not like this world…just as I am not like this world. I am not asking you to take them out of this world…but that you would keep them from evil. They are not of this world just like I am not of this world. Please sanctify (set them apart) by your truth. Your Word is truth."

And Romans 12: 2 "Don't be conformed to this world. Instead, be transformed by the renewing of the way you think…so that you can test and prove God's will for your life, which is good, acceptable and perfect."

Truly, my thinking was changing on a daily basis. It wasn't always easy, but *always* rewarding.

Another lesson happened that remarkably changed the way I thought about fear.

I awoke, startled, in the middle of the night for no apparent reason. As I lay in bed, my husband beside me, my heart pounded. I didn't know why.

Immediately, I asked God, "What's happening? Is something wrong?"

He told me in an authoritative voice, "You will know fear…but no harm will come to you."

"Wha…what did you say?" I had heard Him clearly but I didn't understand.

Silence.
I understood the conversation was over for the time being.

I repeated the phrase. "You will know fear...but no harm will come to you."

What did that mean exactly? Was something awful going to happen to me or my family? Was an intruder inside the house? Is the house on fire?

There were a million "what if's" racing through my brain. The only consolation was the second half of that warning..."no harm will come to you." I truly had to trust God to protect me and my family, no matter what.

I started to get up, but feared that someone was already in the house. They would hear me and come to the bedroom rather than ransack the front of the house and leave us "sleeping". Instead they might bind and gag us and threaten to kill us. There were such people in the world who make victims of the unsuspecting. I had just read Truman Capote's *In Cold Blood* and knew those things could really happen.

I listened intently for any sound that wasn't normal.

The humming of the refrigerator, the tick of the mantle clock, Jeff's slow breathing all seemed magnified. Then I heard something...like a shuffle on the floor. It wasn't pronounced, but I was certain someone was there.

Oh, God! I know you woke me to warn me. I don't dare make a sound. The intruder may kill us all if he knows I'm awake. What should I do?

A scripture from Isaiah 41:10 came to mind. "Don't be afraid. I am with you. Don't be dismayed for I am your God. I will give you strength. Yes, I will help you and hold you up with my righteous right hand."

Gathering courage, I eased out of bed and tiptoed through the bedroom doorway. As I passed the door of the bathroom, I felt a sense of evil inside.

What if I'm not dealing with an evil PERSON, but rather, an evil SPIRIT in my house!

Shivers ran up my spine and out the top of my head. Sweat beads popped out on my face and hands. I didn't know what to do!

With all the courage I could muster, I pushed the door open and clicked on the light. When I opened my eyes to face the demon, nothing was there.

I breathed a sigh of relief and turned to check the rest of the house.
Having done so, and finding no one in the house, I went back to bed and waited until daylight to start my daily routine.

I groggily went to the kitchen and shook off the puzzlement. I would have to wait and see. Maybe I hadn't heard God's "voice" at all.

I packed lunches and sent Jeff off to work, Adam off to school, and bathed baby Nisha. Nothing happened so far. As a precaution, I locked all the doors and windows in the house. I didn't have to be stupid about this. After all…SOMETHING was going to happen to cause great fear! I just believed in my spirit that God had spoken…not Satan.

As the week passed, it got worse. Every time the doorbell rang, I jumped, thinking it might be some stranger trying to entice me to open the door and force his way inside. I'd never used the peephole in the door before, but I began straining to see through it each time the bell rang. To get a better view I'd go to the front room window before opening the door. It was usually only a neighbor dropping by.

If I had a chore outside the house, a grocery trip, or picking up Adam from school it became an ordeal. I carried extra food in the car for Nisha and locked the car doors before pulling out of the driveway. I feared intersections and stop lights where anybody was milling at the corner on the sidewalk. I feared answering phone calls because it might be terrible news. I feared walking to a neighbor's to return a cup of sugar I'd borrowed. Their dog might attack! My nighttime sleeping became sporadic at best. I was fast becoming paranoid, and a nervous wreck.

One week exactly, very early in the morning as suddenly as the first message came, a second message came the same way.

"Ann," the Lord said. "I told you that you would know fear...but no harm would come to you."

"Yes, I know that. I got that part! But WHEN is it going to happen?! I'm sick of waiting for whatever will cause such fear. Let's just get it over with, okay?!!"

"I told you," He said patiently, "You will know fear, but no harm will come to you. That's exactly as you experienced, right?"

I paused and thought. *That's it? That's ALL there is to it? I would KNOW fear...but NOTHING harmful would happen? Is this a JOKE? Well, I don't think it's very funny!*

Quietly, again, He spoke.

"I didn't give you fear. That tactic is always Satan's. In fact, I've told you so. (2 Timothy 1:7) "I have not given you a spirit of fear, but of love, power, and a sound mind." I allowed you to KNOW fear so that you would understand fear and no longer be controlled by it. Fear is never from me. It is from Satan. He uses it as a very powerful control mechanism over people. He uses it to keep them from having the life I want to give them."

He continued. "Whatever you fear is not a reality. It is something you THINK might happen that would harm you. It is like cotton candy. As soon as you bite into it...it melts away. You must realize I do not use fear to manipulate. Satan does.

"But, Lord" I argued, "There are really horrible things that happen to people every day. What if I'm caught in one of those circumstances? Can't I be a victim too? And if it happens, won't I be afraid?"

"You need to know only this" He said. "I AM IN CONTROL. If something actually happens to a child of mine that is unpleasant...I AM STILL IN CONTROL. I will help you deal with that moment and your reactions at that time if you listen to me. I WILL BE IN CONTROL and you can relax in troubled times knowing that I AM. I will give you strength to go through anything. So live your life aware that Satan is the one who places fear in your mind. Fear is NOT from me. Resist his efforts to control you with fear. Know that I am near and will give you the power to overcome your fears. You need never worry.

I thought about what He'd said. Indeed, so much of the fear in my life had been generated by a thought of what COULD happen, not what IS happening.

It all made sense. He allowed Satan to cause paranoia to control me. I had listened to everything Satan told me MIGHT happen and my life was miserable. I had known fear and let it completely ruin my life.

I recalled the times in my life I had passed up good opportunities, or failed to try something new, or didn't voice my opinion because of fear. It was then I decided I would be more aware of Satan's "voice" instilling fear to control me and fight against it.
A wave of peace washed over me. My body seemed to float on a cloud of relief.
God's presence and power were near and He would protect me from all harm. If harm ever came, He

would still keep me under His wings and give me strength to go through it.

"Thank you, God!" I prayed. "How great are your mercies and strong is your might! I really want to be aware of Satan's power of suggestion. Please remind me to test my thoughts against the truth in Your Word and not let fear control."
I was just beginning to "know my adversary" (1 Peter 5:8). "Be alert. Be ever watchful, for your adversary, Satan, is walking about like a roaring lion, looking for someone to consume."

Chapter 21: Garage Sale

During that spring I was able to practice God's concept of the Tupperware bowl. I was cleaning out closets and emptying contents that seemed to multiply in every space available. I wasn't necessarily a hoarder, but I did seem to fill up storage areas without intention. (Is that the same thing?) Maybe there's a little bit of nesting in all of us. Nevertheless, after sorting and deciding to let go of the non-essentials (and that's a relative term) I decided to have a garage sale. Our neighbors found out I was having a garage sale and offered many more items they wanted to dump.

I've never made much money with a garage sale. Maybe I didn't price things well. I loved to shop garage sales. But for all the labor involved, my sales had never been profitable. So, as I was cleaning that spring, I continually asked God what items must go.

His advice: "Whatever you haven't used in the last six months you probably won't use in the next six months. Why are you keeping things that others could be using? Just give it away. The neighbors agreed. They didn't want any of their things back, but to be rid of them.

I will always meet your needs, Ann (Philippians 4:19). If you happen to need something later that you have given away…I'll meet that need too. In the meantime, it will be used instead of deteriorating or going out of style.

That bit of advice made sense to me. So I advertised in the local newspaper a FREE garage sale! I arranged everything neatly on tables and waited for hordes of people to come haul it away. I expected to be finished by noon and start enjoying my clean house immediately.

No one came. I waited until almost noon before the first customers rolled into the driveway. I welcomed them with an enthusiastic smile and said "Thank you for coming. Take anything you want. It's all free."

They wandered through skeptically, selecting a few items and then approached me cautiously.

"We saw your ad in the paper, but thought there would only be junk here. You've got some good stuff. Are you sure it's all free? You could make some money. Don't you want a donation or something?"

"No, thank you," I explained. "My closets were stuffed. I wasn't using any of this." And then I added with a smug smile, "Why should I keep these things when somebody else could be using them?" (Secretly, my pride hoped they would see how "wise" and generous I was.)

They shook their heads in disbelief, thanked me and slowly loaded their cars with their chosen items.

Time after time, people came that day, each with a similar reaction. They were skeptical of the word *free*. They couldn't understand giving away things that had value.

Most took only what interested them leaving plenty behind for others. Some took nothing at all. A few ravaged through like hungry dogs. They packed their cars full with armloads. Still, I had lots left for another day.

On the final day, a nicely dressed older woman came. She approached me holding the ad in her hand. "Is this correct...a *free* garage sale? Are you sure all of this is free? You don't want anything for it?"

"No, but, thanks, anyway." I replied. She shook her head and then began replacing everything she had in her arms.

"I just can't take these things without paying something. That's not right. You have some really nice things and should be paid for it."

I explained to her how I felt about keeping things I was no longer using when others needed them. That made it worse.

"You mean people just come in here and load up and don't offer anything?"

"Oh, yes. It's all FREE. Making money is not what this is all about." I said, hoping she'd get the concept and would not feel obligated.

She only argued more. I knew she really wanted some of the children's clothes for her grandkids, but just couldn't accept a gift. She felt obligated to pay or not take anything. We finally agreed that she would at least pay for the ad in the paper. Then she was satisfied and left with her load.

By end of day, I sat down while no one was around and basked in the good feeling of giving. That alone was enough to make my efforts worthwhile, not considering the relief of getting my house back in order.

Then the Lord gently whispered "My child, I have shown you through this experience the way people respond to my salvation plan. Most take it with reservations…not sure it is really free or that it's really what it's "cranked up" to be. Others take only what they want of it, never seeing how much I have to give them. Some reject my plan of salvation altogether and some are like the lady who couldn't receive it freely. They feel they have to earn it. They can't understand that I have already paid the price so they can have it *freely*. They just don't "get it. Then there are a few who accept it with a ravenous hunger. They accept it gratefully and load up on everything I offer. Most never say "Thank you."

What a beautiful picture He had given me. In a few days He'd shown me much about how people view his plan of free salvation. Salvation from evil within us is something He has already conquered.

Freedom from guilt caused by our sin is part of the salvation He gives to those who believe it. What we do with it is our choice.

(Mark 4: 14-20) "A good farmer sows the Word of God into the hearts of people. Sometimes Satan (like a bird) snatches the truth away from them before it has time to take root.
Others will receive the Word and it will grow for a time, but because they don't believe it much, when trials come to test their faith, they go back to their old ways, not accepting the truth anymore.

Some people receive the Word but are "caught up" in making money and buying things they are too busy to think about it and therefore the truth can't work in their lives.

Then there are a few who receive the Word and use it to produce goodness in their lives. They often increase their kind up to 30%, 60%, or even 100%!"

It was uncanny how often God used mundane things to teach me about Himself. He met me where I was instead of some lofty place of grandeur, though I'm sure He speaks there also. I was eager to learn more.

Chapter 22: Cleaning Floors

It was summertime. Jeff left for work and the kids were still sleeping. Joyously, I grabbed my Bible and sat on the sofa savoring the time I had alone with the Lord. It seemed every day He was teaching me something new.

Sipping my coffee, I was praising Him for all the things He'd done in my life. I then asked Him my daily question. "Okay, Lord...what are our plans for today? I had grown accustomed to allowing Him to organize my daily actions instead of planning them myself. It was amazing how much more I got done by following that plan. I could hardly wait for the day to unfold.

He then reminded me that it was time to strip and re-wax the floor in my kitchen and den area.

Ugh! That's not what I wanted to hear!

The flooring in our house was asbestos tile. Builders used it during the 70's to cut costs. Although it looked lovely when we bought the house, years of use and a product called "Mop and Glow" left it dull and browning around the edges like an old saucepan that had seen better days. The areas that were seldom used had a thick layer of dried "shine-in-a-bottle," which only darkened with age.

He continued saying, "Ann, I want you to deep clean the floor this time. Scrub the old wax off and put a new shine on the floor. I'll help you do it the right way this time."

Inside, I wondered what the "right" way would be. "Right" usually meant more work and time.

Reluctantly, I started sweeping the loose dirt off the floor. At the same time I expected Him to reveal something spiritual to make my effort worthwhile. He didn't disappoint me.

Catching my attention He said, "Did you notice how the floor didn't look very dirty before you started sweeping?"
I had to agree. I kept a pretty tidy house. The areas that were highly noticeable, I kept maintained.

However, after I had swept every hidden corner and places hard to reach, I had a sizeable amount of grit in the dustpan.

He continued, "Sin in your life is like the dirt on this floor. It's seldom noticed until you gather it all up in the light of my Word. For years you never noticed your sin. It was only after you began honestly looking at yourself compared to the person I expected you to be, you saw any sin at all. Instead, you've been comparing yourself to others who looked "more sinful" than you were. If you sweep your heart often, you won't have to deal with a lot of filth. Those who listen to Me closely keep their hearts swept well.

Hmmm, maybe this job won't be so bad after all. Sin really doesn't look so bad until you compare it to His expectations. No wonder it separates us from the fellowship of a Holy God.

"Now," He said. "Let's remove all that old wax."

"But, Lord, I've tried to remove it before. It doesn't come up easily." I began whining, envisioning spending the day on my knees with a paint scraper.

"I never said it would be an easy job," He reminded me, "but I'll help you. I'll give you a formula you don't know that will work. Hardened wax is like a hardened heart. It takes more time to penetrate than one that is cleaned daily."

"So what's this magic formula?" I asked.

"Mix a bucket of hot water with a bottle of rubbing alcohol. Pour it on the floor and let it sit for a bit."

He continued with the illustration. "My love works like that on a hardened heart. It only takes a small amount of my Word to sit in a cynical conscious for awhile. Without distractions to snatch it away, it begins to soften their heart. Couple my Word with consistent love from one of my true believers, and soon their surface crumbles."

Another enlightenment! A hardened heart happens when you don't want to face the truth about your sin. You won't look at it. You ignore it as easily as an area of a floor that you seldom use. It doesn't show much to others, so why bother?

I prepared the magic mix and, to my surprise, it worked! The old wax began dissolving and flaking off the floor. Underneath I could see all the original color I'd forgotten. It was beautiful. I wondered if God saw me as new and beautiful when I dealt with neglected sins.

All this process took several hours but my heart was light as I realized how very dirty my sin had made me. I must've presented quite a challenge for God to undertake. My floor had only taken a few hours to clean, but it would take God years to clean up the mess I'd made of my life. I vowed to let Him clean me entirely, not in part, but in whole. What a blessing I would have missed if I had not cleaned my floor the way God wanted!

The next step was applying the new wax. I dug under the kitchen cabinet and brought out the "Mop and Glow." Then the Lord spoke again.

"Ann, does it make sense to use the same stuff that made your floors so ugly before? That's like a newborn Christian deciding to go back to their old way of living, isn't it? It didn't work before. Why do you think it will work now?"

"But," I asked, "What do I use instead?" I knew He was ready with an answer.

"Paste wax."

Oh, no! I certainly didn't want to hear THAT!

I didn't want to spend all day on my hands and knees. *Isn't there any other way??!!"*

Silence. I knew He would not compromise. It was my choice to obey or not.

The rest of the afternoon was spent hand waxing my floor. Tile by tile, square inch by square inch, I spread Johnson's Paste Wax over the entire floor. All the while I was thinking of the comparisons the Lord had already given me. I wondered how paste wax would fit into the scheme. When I finished the application, and stopped to rest, He spoke again.

"The wax you used on your floor represents the seal I put on my believers in Christ. I actually make you secure and guarantee the Holy Spirit will stay in your heart. Nothing can break that seal, ever. The Holy Spirit will keep your mind and heart sealed until judgment day (Philippians 4: 7).

Wow! What a promise! My security rests in God's power to keep me in His care forever! Why would I ever want to leave?

Then, He continued "Now the floor has to be buffed. The wax seal won't shine unless it is buffed. So, it is with my children. They should know hard trials will come. The fruit of the Spirit comes through experience…practiced by trials. A new believer may not display love, joy, peace, patience, gentleness, humility, goodness, temperance or faith until he has the opportunities to PRACTICE those qualities. Buffing, or trials, provides the opportunity to shine!"

I started my old electric buffer and hummed along while I finished the whole job. It was rewarding to know I was nearing the completion of a task well done. Imagine my surprise when I stepped back and saw no shine.

I was so disappointed. The Lord had guided me through the whole process, yet I had little result for my effort. Maybe it was only the spiritual comparisons He meant to share, but why couldn't He have TOLD me those concepts without all that hard work? I could see little difference in the appearance of the newly waxed floor and the old dirty one.

Then, as if on cue, the sun began to shine through our patio doors. It had been an overcast day until that very moment. When the sun began to shine on my floor, it began to sparkle, reflecting the sunshine.

Very gently God spoke again. "Ann, you must remember, no matter how hard you work at being a good follower, you will never radiate my Spirit until I am allowed to shine through you. You are not the source of light, only the *reflection* of it. I want your "shine" to be on display for all to see so that whatever you do or say, others can see the change in you and say "God really made a difference in her life"(Matthew 5: 16).

My job was done. My day well spent and with it came the reassurance that listening to God's "voice" was so worthwhile.

Chapter 23: Home Again

During our twenty-eight years in Midlothian, Jeff and I both matured individually and as a couple. There were tough times, but many more good times.

Jeff received several promotions at the aircraft company and was eventually made supervisor over the sheet metal department. He was in charge of about two-hundred-fifty workers. Each day was filled with stress and problems that needed solving. He was paid to solve problems and he handled it well.

All the while, he was gaining experience. I was too.

Because my Mom married at age sixteen and finished her high school degree after that, I think she regretted not having a better education. So, she worked to provide us with private lessons in the arts. I think she lived vicariously through us. Maybe all parents do to an extent.

I studied piano for eighteen years, fine art for six years and voice for three years. I'm sure that my skill as a vocalist in high school began much earlier with those lessons. I know the fine art training formed the basis for my career to come.

I resurrected my art work. I started painting again. It wasn't long before I had friends asking for my work. Then, I began getting notice elsewhere. I was approached to teach art to their kids. It wasn't long until adult classes were included. I began making a little money myself, and with that came a sense of worth. And I didn't have to leave home to do it!

Another hobby that also turned into a blessing was refinishing old furniture.

I learned to shop for antique furniture with a dear church friend in Dallas. On Fridays, she and I packed sack lunches and took our kids with us to find all kinds of bargains on very little budget at garage sales. It was such fun, and I'll always be grateful for her friendship.

Eventually I bought pieces that were in need of repair as well as a new finish. So, I struck a bargain with a nearby antique dealer. I would work for him for a low wage in exchange for his teaching me to mend broken pieces. He hired me, and I became a "professional stripper"... (How's THAT title work for you?)...and to top it off...I worked for "tips"!

In the meanwhile, I was also learning to sew for my family. I made most of our garments but always with a pattern. Jeff's mother had been a very fine seamstress who had worked for Herbert Marcus Company in Dallas for years. (Herbert Marcus, Jr. was the brother of Stanley Marcus. Stanley was the retailing genius who expanded his father's specialty store into the famous Neiman-Marcus Company we know today.)

Anyway...she taught me a lot about commercial sewing methods that weren't in over-the-counter patterns.

One day a neighbor lady came to me with a special request. She had made her intended daughter-in-law a wedding dress from a Simplicity pattern. She was pleased that it fit well, but she wanted it to look less homemade and asked if I'd help her with it.

We went to a local store and bought a *Bride Magazine*. There were so many beautiful dresses inside with lots of ideas. We bought some lace, beads, and sequins and I went to work embellishing. My art training made it easy for me to copy.

The finished dress was beautiful. Another neighbor saw my work and asked if I could remodel her daughter's white prom dress into a wedding gown by adding a train. So, I did.

Other work followed when the antique dealer's daughter decided to marry. I created her wedding dress with a special antique lace insert. At that time, I used store-bought patterns to make new creations.

Shortly after, I quit my stripping job and started sewing for the public, full time, from my home. I worked for about five years for word-of-mouth customers for very little pay. I did most of the wedding things on a "gratuity only" basis. At that time, a gratuity was about 10% of the cost. Since the customers usually brought the necessary fabric and notions for me, I just accepted whatever money they gave me as a fair gratuity, not knowing the cost of any of it. All the while, I was getting an education in the garment industry.

I found, however, that most of my customers had no clue how to choose good fabric. They often bought the cheapest goods available and expected my creation to look exactly like the one in the magazine at a fraction of the cost. Well, as my dad used to say, "You can't make a silk purse out of a sow's ear."

So I began searching for retail stores in the Dallas area where I could take the bride and her mom (the one with the checkbook) to purchase the goods I needed to create the gown of her dreams. Once I showed them the difference in quality, they always chose the better products.

However, I dreaded the day we scheduled shopping. My car was not exactly a Cinderella coach. It was a 1973 Mercury Montego Jeff had bought from his brother. Although it was reliable, it sported faded blue paint that had worn through to dull grey on the top. Inside, the headliner had been ripped and was safety-pinned up to keep it out of my face. The seat covers were clean, but threadbare and the right front windshield had been cracked badly by a rock that had bounced off a truck one day on the freeway. I was always embarrassed and apologized for the "ride" as we headed out toward Dallas. My customers were gracious and never seemed to mind as long as *they* didn't have to drive in Dallas traffic.

Anyway, I knew our budget couldn't afford a different car. The one I had was paid for and cost nothing but gas and maintenance. I never even mentioned to Jeff that I longed for a nicer looking car in which to shop with my brides. I simply began asking God for one. I had read in Luke 11: 5-10 an effective way to pray for things when obtaining them seemed impossible.

Jesus spoke about a man who went to his neighbor in the middle of the night to borrow some bread. It seems he had unexpected guests pop in and they were hungry. He needed food and was persistent enough to keep knocking on his neighbor's door until finally his request was granted.

In my childlike faith, I believed if I asked often enough "knocking on God's door, He would give me another car. I really believed it.

So I told God I didn't mind how He wished to give me a better car, I expected Him to do it. I kept repeating that prayer throughout the next few weeks truly expecting it to happen. I never dreamed how God would answer that prayer.

Chapter 24: Car Wreck

The kids and I were on our way to Dallas headed north on a divided highway. The two northbound lanes were separated from the two southbound lanes by a broad grassy median. Crossovers allowed travelers to turn left onto side roads periodically.

It was a clear day and not much traffic at the time. I was taking Adam to his French horn lesson near the center of Dallas and we were going shopping when his lesson was finished.

I was in the right hand lane behind an 18-wheeler cement truck, traveling at a speed of 55 miles per hour. The truck kept slowing down, then speeding up so, I decided to pass. When I was even with its back tires, the driver of the truck gave a blinking left turn signal. I assumed he could see me in his side mirrors, so I pushed the gas pedal to get around him before he started the turn.

Surely, he sees me at his side. He wouldn't turn left from a right hand lane, would he?

But, he did just that. He started turning the monster truck to the left and I started pumping the brakes to get behind him. The momentum of my car at that speed only ignored my braking. In a split second, I had to choose to either hit him head on or try to turn with him.

From the back seat, I heard Adam say, "Mom, we're going to hit him!"

At that time, there was no mandatory law that enforced the use of seat belts in Texas. Most everyone ignored the use of them. They usually were tucked beneath the seat, out of sight and out of mind. I told my kids to brace themselves seconds before the impact and glanced at little Nisha as she slid to the edge of the front seat and pushed against the dash, still holding an old aluminum drinking glass full of ice.

"Oh, God! Take control!" I prayed in my mind as I gripped the wheel and anticipated the force at which we would crash.

The only thing I heard Him say was, "I AM."

I remember the loud crunching noise as our car glanced off the truck's gas tank located underneath the cab and began crawling up the side.
Through my front window, I saw the driver as he shielded his head with his arms, We took off his left front fender and vaulted over the engine in front of his windshield.

I was holding my steering wheel with a "death grip" as the car began descending on the other side of his cab. At the angle of a downward speeding roller coaster, it was headed for a huge concrete culvert at the bottom of which was a collection of rubbish containing several broken beer bottles. I would hit the culvert and nose-flip over and over if I didn't change my wheel direction, but that is not what I thought.

I'd better avoid those beer bottles. They will cut the new tires to shreds and Jeff won't like that.

So, I whipped the steering wheel sharply left and headed straight into the grassy median soaked with morning dew. We slung around in doughnuts several times and just as the car lifted off the ground and began to roll, it hesitated as if held by some power. It slammed down hard in an upright position on an upward embankment, and we finally stopped.

For a few moments, we sat stunned. Then Adam said, "Mom, we'd better get out of here before the car blows!"

I looked up and saw the hood popped open, and billows of white smoke pouring out of the engine. Quickly, we gathered our things and retrieved Adam's French horn from the trunk, undamaged. (*Thank you, Lord!*)

Nisha still gripped the metal cup, now crushed flat. The weakened windshield in front of her face never broke throughout the rough ride. My kids were safe!

A moment later, a young woman, baby on her hip, ran down the incline and asked if she could help. She was traveling behind the truck and saw everything. In fact, she almost hit the truck as he slammed his brakes after the impact. The rear of his truck was still stretched into the highway.

I reassured her we were safe and asked, "Would you mind going back to Midlothian and telling the police we need some help here?" (Cell phones did not exist.) She raced back to her car and did so. I was glad I had a witness in case we needed one later.

The truck driver managed to get his truck over to the side of the road and rushed to us.

"Are you alright, ma'am? I am so sorry. I never saw you at all. You must have been in my "blind spot." You did a hell-of-a-job driving your car through that!"

I looked at his white, pasty complexion, the fear on his face, and his shaky hands. He looked as though he was close to a heart attack. I told him to sit on the bumper and calm down. I assured him we were bruised a few places, but nothing was broken that I could tell.

As we discussed the accident, he said he'd probably lose his job over this one. This wasn't his first accident.

About that time, the paramedics arrived and the state highway patrol. As the cops were getting our statement written and directing traffic around the scene, the paramedics were taking our blood pressure and examining our bruises. The kids and I passed everything fine, but I noticed the truck driver refused to be tested.

A few moments later, one of the officers approached me. "Ma'am, we have arrested the driver of the truck. He is intoxicated. You are fortunate he didn't kill you guys! We'll be able to give you a report as soon as we get him processed and off the streets. We've called a tow truck to pick up your vehicle. He should be here soon."

I looked around. The paramedics had already gone. I asked the officer if he would give us a ride back home.

"I'm sorry, ma'am. We aren't allowed to carry anyone in a squad car with a prisoner. He tipped his hat as he turned to leave. We would now have to wait at the edge of the road until the wrecker arrived.

After the tow man loaded what was left of our car onto his truck bed, I asked him, "Do you mind giving us a ride back home?"

As we squeezed into the cab of his truck, French horn in tow, I saw a white van approaching. It was a friend from our church. She had recognized our car and was stopping to see what had happened. We soon transferred to her car and talked of the accident as she took us back to our house.

The police called later and said they discovered the truck driver had consumed at least ten beers plus medication before driving that morning. We had a case if we wanted to sue for damages.

Our old Mercury was totaled. Besides having four blown tires, the impact was so hard it broke the front axle, yet left us with only a few bruises and an unforgettable experience.

I consulted with a lawyer who told us to get X-rays and let him know if there was any potential permanent body damage. We did and there wasn't. He advised us to settle out of court.

The trucking company sent a representative to see us the next day. She said they intended to compensate us for our trouble. They were sorry the driver had not been more responsible. In fact, he had been fired and was still occupying a jail cell. She offered a generous amount that more than covered the amount we had spent on hospital X-rays and the loss of our car.

With the money offered, Jeff bought our first Cadillac. Gently used, it was a beautiful 1980 brown and tan luxury. Leather, power seats, power windows, built in stereo...the works! God, indeed, gave me more than I dreamed. In the process I learned to be more specific when I prayed, tempering my requests with patience. Now, when I ask God for anything, I always add "if this is what you want for me, instead of "no matter what, this is what I want!"

Chapter 25: Practice Faith

As I continued day by day with my routine, Jeff became more in demand at the aircraft company. It was during this time that he worked seven days a week for four years to meet deadlines during the production of the B1 airplane. His only day off was Christmas day. The money was good, but he was worn down in body and spirit. His time at home was spent keeping up with the bare necessities and sleeping whenever he could relax.

By this time, our kids were much older and involved in activities of their own. Adam had excelled in playing French horn and performed with the Dallas Youth Orchestra. Each summer, he attended music camp at Interlochen Center for the Arts in Michigan, which furthered his efforts and set his determination to become a professional musician. His senior year in high school, he won the National Seventeen Magazine Competition. This helped pay for his first year at New England Conservatory of Music in Boston, where he earned his performance degree.

Nisha was becoming a beautiful young lady, popular with her school mates. Her bubbly personality and compassionate spirit produced a large friend base in her pre-teen world.

During those years, I obtained my retail license and learned buying wholesale. From my home I retailed formalwear fabrics, notions, and laces and invested in a re-built commercial sewing machine with the profit.

I gained enough confidence to charge more for my labor. The work was pouring in. I learned to create patterns from pictures and ideas. My reputation as a seamstress was reaching beyond Midlothian without advertising. Every job I completed furthered my skills and education, producing referrals from my customers.

There were times it was costly, like the time I dressed six bridesmaids, one of which was overweight. She decided to go on a starvation diet two weeks before the wedding. When she came for her final fitting the day before the wedding, her dress hung loosely. She had lost seventeen pounds by eating nothing but lettuce and water! I had to remake the garment in two days, all the while practicing grace!

There were several times that catastrophe struck, but God gave me direction to get through each ordeal. One catastrophe I remember well.

It was a warm spring day. Workspace was limited to my living room, so I hung a completed wedding dress from a door facing and draped the train on an upholstered chair close by. I sat on the floor and rested my back against it while working on another order. The finished dress was to be picked up in a few days.

I was wearing a faded red blouse that I had washed many times, yet somehow my perspiration caused the faded red dye to bleed on the bottom of the train. I was mortified to see the faint red stain there. What was I going to do??!!
For the rest of the morning, I gently tried to wash the stain out of the polyester satin gown by spot cleaning with everything from Spray and Wash to diluted bleach.

I began to worry that the shiny finish on the fabric would soon lose its sheen. I was praying hard for God would tell me what to do. Then, the doorbell rang.

"Good morning, Ann." It was my neighbor lady who came for her daily visit.

Nanny (as we in our neighborhood called her) was in her seventies and finished her daily chores early in the morning. She came to my house to visit on a daily basis. She didn't mind my working as she talked.

I explained to her the calamity of the day and she said, "Have you tried buttermilk and salt?" I had never heard of such, but she explained that old remedy worked years ago on the farm.

What did I have to lose? I mixed a portion and dabbed it on the satin. Then, as she had instructed, I hung the dress (covered well in a garment bag except for the stained area) on the clothesline outside my kitchen window. As the sunshine warmed the stain, it began to disappear.

Thank you, God! He had come to the rescue again!

Another day, an employee was trimming tulle layers under a completed wedding gown as I was sewing up another one. The dress had sixteen layers of tulle ending with a lace-embellished top layer of chiffon.

She came to the room where I was sewing, scissors in hand, a look of despair on her face. She hesitated a moment and then confessed. "I cut through the top layer of the gown by mistake."

The bride was to pick up her dress that afternoon!

I breathed a prayer that God would help me ACT calmly and not say anything that Satan could use to cause guilt or blame. I was beginning to recognize opportunities to *practice* patience (which is, learning to wait without getting frustrated), even if the occasion would merit otherwise.

I rose from my machine to inspect the damage and found that the cut was close to a seam. I could remove about four inches of width in that panel of the skirt and taper the loss into the original seam. It would take about two hours, but I had the time to do so before the bride came.

Time after time, the Lord was changing me by giving opportunities to ACT like I possessed spiritual fruit even if I didn't FEEL that way. Eventually, those practice sessions produced the real fruit in me. I was learning to control the automatic reactions that for years had dominated my being. I was learning to kill my old sinful nature.

(Galatians 5: 22) "But the fruit of the Spirit is love, joy, peace, patience, gentleness, goodness, faith, humility, and temperance and there is NO law against those things.
    If you belong to Christ, then you have destroyed your old nature with its affections and inordinate desires. If you possess the spirit of Christ, then ACT like it!" (ACT until it is FACT!)

(Romans 6:8-14) "If you are a true believer, you will recognize the person you used to be was crucified with Christ. Your old sinful nature was given a fatal blow. Therefore, you shouldn't continue to serve it. If you are dead to your selfish nature, then you are free from being controlled by it.

If we believe we are dead with Christ, then we also believe we are resurrected with him.

When Christ was raised from the dead, He conquered death, and now He lives forever for God's purposes.

Therefore, we should reason that we are dead to sin and alive unto God for His service because of the empowerment through Christ.

Don't let sin control you anymore. You don't have to obey your temptations. Your eyes, hands, feet and minds don't have to do things that are sinful anymore.

So, give yourself to God's service and become righteous. For sin should not have power over you anymore. You are not being "good" because you HAVE to... but because you WANT to."

Chapter 26: God Meets My Needs

Eventually, from my home, I included the sale of formal invitations, dyed shoes, jewelry, tuxedo rental, silk flowers, wedding veils and hats, and catering in my product line. My savings was growing and my work was taking over our house. So, I considered moving my work area from my house to a different place.

I moved to a storefront in 1985 and called it "The Fairy Godmother." A friend of mine who did floral work from her home joined me and we split the rent and utilities. It was with much faith and apprehension that we signed the one-year lease. Rental was $600 per month! Both of us trusted the Lord to bring in the money. Jeff and her husband joked as they built fixtures for the store that they would need an armored truck to haul our earnings to the bank.

I thank the Lord for the experience of my twenty-one year career. What started as a hobby, God turned into a business that gave so much. I learned to work with people and meet deadlines. (No bride wants her dress the day AFTER the wedding!) I worked under stress and learned to listen closely to others. The most valuable lesson I learned, however, was to trust God all the more.

There were several visual lessons God gave me during that time which affected the way I live today.

About a year after we opened the store, my friend "bailed out" due to illness in her family and left me with the balance of the lease. Business was good, but not good enough to keep up the money demands. Little by little my bank account was dwindling.

"Lord, I have $28 in the bank. I told you when I started this business it belonged to you. If you want me to fold, just let me know. Otherwise, YOU have a big job to do today. The rent's due tomorrow and I don't have $600. I know you are aware of that, but I'm wondering what you are going to do about it?"

No answer. We already discussed this issue before several times in the past. He told me He would meet ALL my needs according to His riches in Christ Jesus (Philippians 4: 19). I believed Him…BUT…this was a very big trust challenge.

I closed the cash drawer and prepared for my last consultation that day.

Jan was a grocery checker at a nearby store. I wasn't expecting much from her even if she decided to invest the "half down, balance-upon-completion" stated on my contract.

She entered the door with a bright smile, a pretty girl full of expectation. I smiled back, but inside I was distracted by my worry. (I think there's another description for that…LACK of TRUST in God!

We sat down at the round table and I saw she had a *Bride Magazine* in her hand. As was my custom in a consultation, I listened closely to a bride and her desires. Then I drew a sketch of the dress she wanted copied from a magazine. From the sketch I made a list of supplies, and gave her a written bid.

If she agreed to the price, she would pay half of the estimate. I would then schedule her fittings. Brides came for three fittings and left with their final product when satisfied. I guaranteed my work.

"Let's see, Jan, which of these beauties do you want?" I mounted my glasses just so and examined the picture she laid in front of me. It was a gown by Demetrios, a top designer of the time, and I knew that particular gown retailed for more than $3,000.

I often had girls with "champagne taste and a beer budget" expecting me to provide the same thing for much less and often I did, but I always had to downgrade the quality of the goods involved. I would change the silk to taffeta or synthetic satin, chose a lesser expensive lace, fewer beads and was able to get within their budget, not losing the look of the gown they wanted. So, I began that approach.

"That's a beautiful choice, Jan. Do you want your dress exactly like this one, or modified?" I knew the bountiful use of Alençon lace on this dress was really going to escalate the price.

"No, ma'am, exactly like this one," she said. In my

mind, I was thinking I would go through the motions, give her an estimate, and then do it all again to fit her budget, which I anticipated by experience would be a LOT less.

Routinely, I filled in the information on the estimate sheet...yardage, amounts, costs, labor, then I handed her the final estimated price. She took the paper and I waited for surprise to spread over her face as predictable as the sun coming up in the morning. The final tab was $2,400.

She smiled a great big smile, pulled out her checkbook and wrote me a check for $1,200. I was dumbfounded. The Lord had come through just in time to pay the rent and enough extra to buy supplies for the gown.

I flipped open the calendar to schedule her pattern fitting as she explained why her decision was so easy. It seemed she saw one of my bride gowns three years earlier and decided to start saving so that I could make her gown too. What an angel! She didn't have any idea she was, indeed, my angel for the day and that God prepared her to meet my need three years earlier!

That evening, after she left and I was locking the front door of the shop, I thanked God again for His faithfulness to His word. I remembered that "We are not self-sufficient…and shouldn't even think we are. Our sufficiency lies in God" (2 Corinthians 3:5). I still had so much to learn.

Chapter 27: Secrets Revealed

There were more than a few times the Lord would reveal things to me that were totally inconceivable, things that were impossible for me to know except for His "voice". Some people call that skill "extra sensory perception" or ESP, but I just listened for His "voice."

After dancing circles all week to meet the deadlines for several special occasions, I was back at the store/workshop on a Sunday afternoon trying to finish a "mock" for a bride that had an appointment early the next day.

The mock dress was cut from inexpensive unbleached muslin. Nothing pretty to look at but it enabled me to give my customer a three dimensional "sketch" of her dress before I actually cut into the more expensive cloth. It also provided me with a cloth pattern that was sculpted to her body and fit her perfectly. I was able to make changes easily by snipping here, tucking there and literally gave her choices she could not make as decisively any other way. From the cloth pattern I made all the revisions on a paper pattern for her dress. From this, I cut the fabric for her gown.

This particular bride chose a contemporary gown from *Modern Bride Magazine*. It had a straight skirt with cascading ruffles attached to the sides that blended into the train at the back of the gown. The ruffles were not co-operating.

I studied the picture and worked for several hours experimenting with different cuts, trying to get the look she wanted. Nothing was working.

Usually, because of my art training, I could look at a picture and know what cut was needed to control the behavior of the fabric, but in this case I was "stumped." I had already cut almost ten yards of muslin and had all kinds of cast-off ruffles lying at my feet.

I slumped in my chair, chin in hands and asked God what to do. I never had such a difficult time cutting a mock before.

"Father, I know YOU know how I should cut this ruffle. I've already tried everything I know. The bride will be here first thing in the morning and I must have this ready. Please, PLEASE help me! Tell me how to cut this ruffle so that it will cascade like it does in this picture!"

I waited for what seemed a long time. Just as I was starting to fold up the mess on the floor, He spoke.

"Cut a doughnut, Ann."

"Cut a doughnut?? Did I hear you right, Lord??...a doughnut???"

I knew His silence meant He expected me to listen and listen well. He knew I heard Him. There was no need to repeat anything. (Oh, we'd do well to learn that trick with our own children!)

So I did. I cut a very large doughnut. Then I sliced through one side and held it up by the inner edge. It fell beautifully into the kind of ruffle I had tried so hard to make.

"Thank you, God!!" I squealed in delight. "Truly you are the Revealer of secrets! All kinds!"

(Daniel 2:22) God reveals the deep, secret things. He knows what we cannot see and all knowledge and truth lives with Him.

I really loved the work I did. There was such reward in seeing a young woman elated with the way she looked in her wedding gown. She glowed when she slipped into her new gown and all the more on her wedding day.

I was so blessed to be a part of that. I really took for granted the skill God had given me.

Often, however, I wondered why He led me into that particular business. It seemed a bit trite that so much money was spent on a wedding that could be used in other more pertinent ways, or so I thought. One day, He showed me why.

Chapter 28: Why Weddings?

It was raining…pouring down. (What is it about me and the rain?)

Anyway, I was coming home from buying groceries and took a left turn onto an entrance ramp to the freeway. Suddenly, my car whirled into hydroplane. Naturally, I gripped the wheel and tried to turn the car onto the ramp instead of into the ditch where I was headed. Oh, and I stomped the brakes too! Not good.

Fortunately the cars behind me stopped while I did my "car ballet". There was no one else involved.

I landed someplace on the ramp that wasn't covered in water because the car slowed and stopped just before I would have plunged down a deep incline.

Red-faced and shaken, I slowly straightened the car and proceeded onto the freeway, and thanked God I hadn't been injured. Little did I know He had given me a "practice run" for what was about to happen.

I had been in the wedding business almost twenty years. One of the services I rendered was tuxedo rental for all the guys involved in the wedding. Unlike most stores that told the guys "Just pick up your tux a couple of hours before the wedding. Everything will fit fine."(Rarely does that happen!)…I brought all those tuxedos to the church an hour before wedding rehearsal and personally fit each fellow at no extra charge. There were always some parts of the unit that did not work well. I measured accurately, but that did not guarantee the warehouse employee had an alert mind when he filled the order.

That extra service allowed me time without stress to alter or exchange the things that didn't fit well *before* wedding day.

So, the evening of my "sliding episode" I had dressed sixteen guys at the rehearsal for a wedding that started at 4:30 the next afternoon. True to form, there were shoes that had to be exchanged and cuffs on coats and pants that needed altering. I took the parts that didn't fit and knew I had a trip the next morning to the tux warehouse to pick up the replacement items and then bring them back to the church before the ceremony began.

I woke up early in the morning. The rain was still pouring and the radio was warning me to stay indoors unless it was absolutely necessary to be on the road. Flood stages were already in effect, but in the wedding business and funeral business (lots of similarities) the "show" must go on.

I loaded the car with all the exchange pieces and traveled forty-five minutes via a busy four-lane highway across Dallas to the tux warehouse.

The warehouse had my replacement order ready when I arrived. Now, all I had to do was deliver the goods to the church, place them in each guy's bag and I'd be off the rest of the day. God had different plans.

About twenty minutes away from the church, I cautiously traveled at about forty miles per hour behind a lot of other vehicles. I thought I'd have better vision if I could only get around the semi in front of me. The rain was coming down in sheets. I couldn't see "diddly". I checked my rear view mirror and accelerated to get around him. I was not going more than fifty-five miles per hour when I became airborne, or rather, water-borne. I was hydroplaning again!

At least, this time, I remembered to relax my grip on the wheel and let the car go its own way. So in Saturday morning Dallas traffic, on a four-lane highway packed with cars, I proceeded to "doughnut" around and slide across two lanes into the center guard rail going backwards. The car continued its momentum all the while scraping the whole right side of my car so forcefully that I saw sparks flying. I had seen that kind of action when I was a child and watched my dad working metal on a grinder in his shop.

Little by little, I pumped the brakes just enough to get control and eventually managed to stop against the rail. All the while I was praying, "Oh, Jesus, please, please, PLEASE take control of this car!" So, He did. There's NO way (my family will attest to this) I was *that* good a driver.

I sat behind the wheel staring into the traffic facing me. All four lanes were zipping by. No one stopped to help. It was all very dangerous. There was no way I could turn around and get into the flow of the traffic at a speed fast enough. Besides, I wasn't sure the car was able to function. I had no cell phone. What was I to do?

I grabbed my purse and umbrella and locked the car doors. The tuxedos were still hanging on a rod over the back seat. I had to find a tow truck.

I crawled over the center rail and stood there waiting for somebody to pity me and help. That wasn't happening. So, I raised both hands over my head and stood there like a statue! If nothing more, someone would call a "paddy wagon" and haul me to the nearest psycho ward. Two seconds later a couple of guys in a pickup truck wheeled over to my rescue.

Now, don't think for one moment the thought didn't enter my mind they were escaped convicts ready to take me into high grass, molest my body, shoot me and feed me to the buzzards. I just had to trust God that He knew what He was doing, and I'd be fine.

They took me to the nearest car dealership and dropped me off. I thanked them and offered to pay, but they said they were only glad to help. What a nice place to be. Texas still had white-hat cowboys in trucks that would help anybody.

I called a tow truck and in ten minutes climbed into it and met Randy, my $75-per hour knight-in-not-so-shining armor.

He nodded his head toward me as he whipped the vehicle in reverse.

"We gotta hurry, Ma'am. They've green-tagged everything on the roads today. A cop was side-swiped and killed yesterday 'cause of all this rain. So, they gotta have all stalled cars off the road ASAP." That meant, in layman's terms, that all cars were fair game for any tow truck to pick up. Normally, if a car is red-tagged, only the tow trucks that were sanctioned by the county could pick up a stranded auto. Mine was like a juicy steak to all tow truckers that day. If we were too late, my car would be gone.

It was…along with all the tuxedos that were to be worn at 4:30 pm for wedding pictures. The wedding didn't start, however, until 6:00 pm. By now, it was 12:30 pm.

Mentally, I prayed, *"Oh, dear Lord! Now what??!!"*

Randy, my knight, was also my angel for that day. He told me exactly what I should do.

"Looks like somebody got your car already. I tell you what. I'll take you to a rental car place a few blocks from here and you can rent a car to get around in. They'll have a phone too, so you can call and find out where they took your car. It'll either be in Dallas or Garland…'cause your car was right on the county line. Oh, and you'll need three things to get your car out of the pound… eighty dollars, CASH. (I had that) your driver's license (I had that) and proof of insurance. Ooops! It was locked in the glove box of the car!

I also needed proof of insurance to *rent* a car!

I called home. My daughter answered the phone. She was moving home from college for the summer and was between trips from her apartment north of Dallas. It was a miracle she was there at that particular time, but what's new?

When she answered the phone I blurted out, "Honey, look inside the file cabinet under insurance and fax me a copy of our current insurance card. I've wrecked the car and need to rent another.

"Mom, are you okay??!! I could hear the anxiety in her voice.

"Oh, I'm fine, but I need a car in a hurry. I'll explain later, sweetie."

After hearing I had no injuries to my body, she did what I asked and in thirty minutes I had proof of insurance in hand and a car rented.

While waiting for her to send the fax, I called the Garland impound station and sat through a fifteen-minute busy signal only to be told they did not have my car. So, I was off to the downtown Dallas car pound. It was still raining hard.

When I finally parked and got out of the car, I noticed my hair was stuck to my face and my clothes soaked. Not too impressive, but that was the least of my concern. I looked up and found there was a waiting line out the door of the facility. Apparently, I was not the only one who had "car trouble" that day. I became number fifteen in line.

I thought surely a wedding emergency would take precedence over the rest of the cases in front of me, so I pushed my way through the crowd to the front of the line, all the while apologizing and explaining my rudeness.

When I reached the counter behind glass I said, "Excuse me, miss, I have a real emergency. You see my car hydroplaned and was impounded about an hour ago. It was full of tuxedos going to a wedding that will begin in only 3 more hours. I really don't need my car. I only need to get the tuxes out of the car, and I'll come back Monday and pick up my car."

She lifted her weary eyes and with a dour expression said, "Get to the end of the line. There are ABSOLUTELY NO mediating circumstances!"

I retreated, very embarrassed under the glower of all the others in line. I knew what they were thinking. "She ain't got no wedding. She's just trying to break in line!" They nudged together tighter as I took my place at the end of the line, which by then, had grown by three more people!

As we all stood helplessly time-bound, we began discussing our plights. They had overheard my wedding story and were eager to share how their weddings had "goofy" things happen too. I listened and we chatted more.

Those in line who didn't want to get involved with strangers were listening to our talk like some daytime soap opera. Then, I happened to mention what the tow truck fellow told me.
"Did you know that you are required to have 3 things to get your car out of here?...a driver's license, proof of insurance...and $80 CASH."

I think "cash" was the magic word. One by one the line dwindled to four people. I was now number three!!

When I stepped up to the counter the second time, she took my information and made a phone call. All the while the minutes were ticking by.

Then, she looked up all deadpan and said, "Your car's not here. Consider it stolen. There's a pay phone in the corner if you want to report it stolen. Thank you...NEXT."

Stunned, I located the phone, called the police and reported the theft. Things were not supposed to be this hard.

"Lord, are you getting the picture here?" I prayed under my breath. "It is necessary that I have tuxes on sixteen bodies in perfect order in less than three hours and I haven't got SPIT! HELP!!"

I decided I'd start all over again, so I called the tux warehouse to re-order the missing parts. By then, the rain was subsiding and I might make it in time. Then I was told by the order clerk there was a problem.

"I'm sorry, Mrs. Norris, but there are no other parts for that style tuxedo." We gave you all the extra parts available this morning. This is prom season. We don't have any more in the warehouse of that particular style.

"Okay," I told him. "Just give me sixteen new units in another style…all black. I'll be there in thirty minutes to pick them up."

I then called the bride and told her, " I've had a "little car trouble" and might be a bit late with the exchanges…but not to worry…I would BE there.

"Oh, and I upgraded your tux order. The warehouse ran out of your chosen style, so I'm giving you 16 more expensive tuxes at no extra charge. Will you please have your guys ready to change their coats and pants when I get there? I will alter them on their bodies if need be. Have the photographer start with the girls if you will, and, Honey, don't you fret at all.

I've never missed a wedding deadline and I'm not about to start now! Everything will be just fine."

I hoped she didn't hear the panic in my voice. I was beginning to wonder how God was going to make this work.

I left the warehouse at 4:15 pm. It took another half hour to get to the church. The guys ran out to the car and helped unload everything. Soon they were dressed again and waiting for pictures. I had to alter a couple of pair of pants and one coat sleeve. God was good! The bride was radiant, spirits at the wedding were joyful, and I felt relief flow into my body.

All the way home, I kept questioning *"WHY??" What was this all about? Where was my car?* My body was still so tense it tingled. Yet, I knew God had orchestrated the whole day. (Romans 8:28...For we know that ALL things work together for the good of those who love the Lord...those who are called according to His purposes.) But I didn't know what lesson He wanted to reveal and He wasn't ready to tell me yet.

I returned home in the rental car about 5:30 pm. Jeff met me as I drove into the driveway.

"Nisha told me what happened, honey. Are you alright? Where is the car?"

I hated to tell him I didn't know. It wasn't good news at all, but I knew God was in control of the whole day and reassured Jeff of that. I went into the house, kicked off my heels and changed my wet clothes. My body was still tied in knots from the tension of the day. I took two Tylenol, drank a glass of milk and tried to calm down.

I related the whole story to Jeff as we sat at the kitchen table. He was just thankful I hadn't been killed. After we went to bed he held me close as I cried myself to sleep. I guess that was a natural reaction considering what I'd been through.

At 2:00 am, I awoke. When thoughts of the previous day rumbled through my head, I decided to slip into the kitchen and make a pot of coffee. While waiting for it to brew, I called the Garland pound again to ask if, by chance, my car had been found. (At 2:00 am there was no busy signal.) The clerk was able to find my car immediately. It seems they had it all along. The paperwork hadn't "caught up" with the car when I called previously, so they didn't know it was there.

"Thank you, Lord!" ran across my lips. So, with coffee and my Bible in hand, I headed to the den to have a little "discussion" with God.

In the quietness of the moment, when I was calm enough to hear Him, he gently said, "Ann, I know you want to know why I allowed such calamity yesterday. So now I will tell you."

He continued, "Weddings are a picture of my coming back to earth for my church. My intentions are for every wedding to represent that, but most every wedding Satan tries his best to mess up that picture. That's usually why most weddings include something catastrophic. Just wait till the REAL thing happens. When I come for my bride (the true believers), all chaos will break loose. That's why I've told my believers to be alert.

Pay attention to the signs of the times I told you about in Matthew 24 and 25. Stay in touch with me and each other moment by moment…even more so as the day of my approaching gets nearer"(Hebrews 10:25).

It is YOUR job to help make every wedding run smoothly so that the example of my coming doesn't get messed up."

I cried softly as I realized after all those years in the wedding business I finally knew my real purpose. Before then, I often looked at the money spent, the hours of planning and the frazzled emotions of families only to think that it was all such a frivolous waste. Many times I wondered if I couldn't serve the Lord better doing something else for His glory.

In His kind way, He knew I needed to learn much about myself and Him through the business. Indeed, it was HIS business, not mine. I was glad He finally revealed the purpose for serving Him there.

Matthew 25: 1-12… "The coming of the kingdom of heaven is like this:

There were ten maids invited to be ready for the wedding festivities. All were supposed to meet the groom when he called them to go to the wedding, whether day or night. The time was unannounced, so their lanterns were to be filled with oil at all times and ready whenever he called.

Five were prepared. Five were not.

Because the groom was later than they thought, all sense of expectation was gone.

Then, suddenly in the night, they heard the call and began scrambling to dress, ready their lanterns, and go.

"Please", said the maids who weren't as prepared to the maids that were ready," lend us some of your oil. Our lamps have gone out!"

"No way!" said the five who were prepared. "Go to the oil vendor and buy your own!"

So, they did, but while they were gone, the groom

passed by and the five prepared maids went joyously to the wedding. After they arrived the doors were locked and nobody else could join the party as was the custom.

"Please, please, let us in!" cried the late maids who had not been ready when he knocked on their door.

The groom simply replied, "Of course not. I don't even know who you are."

Jesus finished the story by saying "Be watchful, because nobody knows the day or hour when I shall come again."

Chapter 29: God Yells!

There was only one time during my period of recognizing God's voice that He ever spoke loudly. You must realize I am *not* talking about hearing audibly. The voice I heard was always thoughts in my mind, but the ideas were not things I could have known without the "voice" of God talking to me. I hope I'm making that clear.

In general, I learned to decipher God's voice from Satan's by their different approach. Satan would use ideas tainted with urgency, such as, "You'd better hurry and do this or this is going to happen!" He would also mix scripture with lies, trying to deceive me.

Whereas, God was always more gentle and subtle, saying, "I want you to do this, Ann. He called my name often. He always spoke in a calm, quiet way (James 3:17). "But the wisdom from God is first pure, then peaceable, gentle and easy to entreat. It is full of mercy and good actions. Fair to all and has no deceit."

So, it was surprising to me that God would ever use His voice in any other way, but, I'm glad He did. Let me explain.

It was Thursday, the one weekday (other than Sunday) that I closed the store and used the time to pick up supplies, buy groceries, and take care of all the needs of my family and business. It was always a compelling day.

I was on my way to be with a friend who asked me to hold her hand during breast biopsy. She needed support, so I promised I'd meet her at the clinic.

On the way, I had to pick-up some rhinestone buttons that were "on hold" at a fabric store. I called the store clerk earlier that morning and instructed her to have the order ready, so I could get them quickly.

The store was in Oak Cliff, very near downtown Dallas. Past its heyday, it still bore the storefronts common in the 1940's and 1950's. But it had become a shopping area for those of low income and bargain hunters…a great area to find good prices but still a high-crime area.

It was noon when I arrived and the sun was shining brightly. There were more people loitering on the sidewalks than shopping. Most were men with unshaven faces and tattered clothing.

I parked next to a beat-up old car, windows rolled down, where two men sat smoking.

Normally, I would lock my car doors the moment I left my car, but on that day, being in a rush, I didn't.

I ran inside the store, picked up the buttons, thanked the clerk for her help and darted back outside.

In my peripheral vision, I noticed a huge man leaning against the outside of the building in front of my car. I did not make eye contact but proceeded to step off the high curb and opened my car door. I could hear the two men in the car next to me laughing and talking rapidly in Spanish. The moment my back touched the driver's seat, I heard God's voice.

"LOCK IT!"

Without hesitation, I reached the automatic lock and pushed hard. I heard the mechanism click into place at the same time I saw the big man grasping the handle of my car door.

To this day, I wonder what would have happened if I had not been "in tune" with the Lord that day.

I suppose, because my assailant's efforts were foiled, he energetically screamed curses at me as I backed out of the parking space.

"You bitch! You think you're better 'n me 'cause you drive a fancy Cadillac?! It don't matter none! I drive a Cadillac a lot newer than your piece of trash!"
On and on, he ranted, turning the air blue as I drove off. It was like the demons of Hell occupied his body.

I was shaking, but in awe of the protection my Heavenly Father gave me. He was right about the "fear" thing. When you are in a circumstance that should be terrifying, you are too busy *doing* to be afraid. It was *after* the incident, I realized I was too busy locking the door and getting out of there to be afraid. God was right, and He proved it.

Chapter 30: Knowing Myself

Jeff and I became involved in the community through our church, our neighborhood, and the kids' school activities. We were making new friends everywhere. I met one of those friends through participating in a theater production.

During Adam's senior year in high school, the band was earning money for a trip to Florida to perform in the Orange Bowl Parade. Some of the parents decided to present a play as a fund raiser. I joined the group.

We had such fun doing that play, we decided to continue with another production…and another…and another. It was the beginning of Midlothian Community Theater which is active today. Through that venture I met Kitty.

Kitty was a squatty lady who had no family. She lost all her family, except one niece by the time she was forty-two, shortly before I met her.

Kitty was depressed and angry with God for taking all her loved ones. I noticed her sadness and prayed God would provide an opportunity to speak with her about her spiritual condition. It was on that first play set I recognized my opportunity during a break at rehearsal.

She sat alone in an area off-stage. I approached her with a smile and determination to discern just the right time to say something about her condition. She had been crying.

I gently touched her shoulder and said, "Kitty, I've noticed you are terribly sad. I know you lost your mother a few months ago, but I sense there's something more troubling you. Then I ventured, "How long has it been since you had a good relationship with God?"

It shook her visibly that I'd been that perceptive, if a bit presumptuous, (as Pastor Robert Williams had been with me). She looked up through her tears and said with a distant look in her eyes "A long, long time. Since I was a teen-ager, I guess."

We only had a few minutes to talk before rehearsal resumed, but I had the chance to invite her to come to my house and talk soon.

It wasn't that Kitty had no friends. She was very active in her church. She was their bell choir director. In fact, her parents had been charter members of the church she attended. She had been in church all her life, yet never knew God in a personal way. Her social life revolved around her church activities but she was walking a two-sided life. Just like me, she had learned the behavioral patterns that kept her "little secret" safe in her social circle. She had "Church-ianity" not Christianity.

I told her I could see the anger she still held for God. She hid that fact so deeply that she had trouble recognizing it. She hungered for anyone to listen to her. She began coming often to our house and we began a study in the book of Romans. It was amazing to see the truth of God penetrate her heart. It was easy for her to sit through sermons on Sunday and not allow the Holy Spirit to speak to her heart. It was a big difference to read the Word alone and discover the truth. Like a mirror, the scriptures showed her as she really was.

That next spring, at Easter time, Kitty finally met God on His terms. She was driving down the freeway when she realized that Christ had died for *her*. She told me she wept so much she had to pull over and get out of traffic. After that, Kitty became a part of God's family...and ours.

She was always bringing gifts as she entered the door: New tea towels for me, a book, music tapes for us to enjoy. She loved us, and it showed. Little by little, I saw Kitty change into a different person. She looked the same year after year, but she softened, became less cynical, less angry, and more interested in learning Biblical principles *and* less depressed.

It was Kitty who introduced me to books by Frank Minirth and Paul Meier, physiologist and psychiatrist who wrote from a Christian angle during the 70's and 80's. Their books, *Love is a Choice, Happiness is a Choice* and *Imperative People* helped me discover why I was so angry for many years. Their viewpoints helped me understand myself. Because of my past experience with psychiatrists, I simply read a lot of self-help books written by professionals. It helped me look at myself from a different perspective and change the things I could. By applying their principles and talking to God about my condition I was able to accept who I was, warts and all, working toward improvement.

Years of research and experience have brought the science of psychiatry a million miles from where it was. I don't discourage anyone from seeing a professional, but I educated myself and learned to lean on God as my counselor. Through His guidance it worked for me. I probably wouldn't have discovered this great counseling had it not been for my friend, Kitty.

She died of diabetes and heart failure at age 57.

Chapter 31: The New House

In the early 80's, Dallas was exploding with people moving to Texas for better employment. This spurred the building glut in Midlothian. Houses were popping up all over our little town. It was a productive time.

With Jeff's increase in pay through his many overtime hours and the sale of our little house in Dallas, we decided to buy a bigger house, one we could use for entertaining and enjoying all our friends.

Adam was in college and only home for the summers, while Nisha was just entering her teen years with an abundance of friends. My business was booming, too. We felt we needed more space and could afford it then.

We looked all over Midlothian for a new house. My love for antiques drew me to older homes, two-story, quaint, but most of those needed too much repair. Jeff's practicality drew him to new homes with far less maintenance.

We were looking one Sunday afternoon when we drove into a new division several miles south of town. The builders had created a small restricted development that was so attractive. The homes sat on one or two acres with lots of space between them. Jeff was smitten and so was I.

The house we loved was about 2,700 square feet. It had a porcelain-tiled foyer with a formal octagonal dining room to the right. Straight ahead was a huge living room with a gorgeous Victorian-style fireplace with a beveled mirror overhead. High above, was a beautiful 6'x6' stained glass skylight. An expensive Casa Blanca fan hung from the center of the skylight mounted on heavy oak beams. Decorative wood trim iced the fully wood- paneled room and added grace.

Although the three-bedroom, two-and-a-half bath was new, it had the rich flavor of being from an era long past when detail was very important. The builder had done exquisite work.

I was in awe...*and* "in LOVE!" It truly was a beautiful home for someone, but we just looked at the price tag and sighed.

Jeff was impressed too, but the price was staggering even to our newly inflated budget. We pretty much left thinking *somebody else* would own this beautiful house.

We continued searching, but never found anything that suited both of us.

We then had the idea to buy some land nearby and have our house built within our budget. So, I called the builder who had built the house we loved to ask if he would build one for us.

Diana, his wife, answered the phone. Because their daughter was in the same grade as Nisha in school, we were already acquainted.

"Hi, Diana, this is Ann Norris. How are you doing?" As customary, I chatted about trite things until I got to the point.

"Is Mike there so I could talk with him about building Jeff and me a new house?"

"No, Ann, Mike's not here right now, but may I help you? Do you know what kind of house you want?" (Diana was well-versed in Mike's business).

I told her we'd seen Mike's work in the "ultimate dream house" and loved it, but the price was over our budget. We decided to find a lot and have Mike build a house within our budget. We were looking at much smaller square footage.

To my surprise, Diana said, "Ann, if you are really interested in the house on Cripple Creek, we could make you a deal you can't refuse. You can have that house for what it would cost now to build a smaller one. Mike has built so many houses this year and sales are beginning to drop off. We really need to move our "spec" homes. The interest is killing us."

Wow!! That was something I wasn't expecting!

I told her I thought we were definitely interested, but I'd have to talk with Jeff first.

Of course Jeff was also excited about the possibility of getting the house, but we had to get financing. In the meantime, Diana gave us the keys to our dream home and placed an "under contract" sign out front.

Each afternoon, we drove out to the new house and walked through it again and again. We never dreamed when we were first married that we'd ever own anything as nice. God was gracious, and we knew He sent the opportunity.

Financing, however, was a different story. We tried several places to borrow the money to buy the house but most financial institutions were refusing our request because Jeff's base salary was not enough. Our three year inflated income was due to his overtime work. It was not a "regular" income. They kept requiring more and more down payment.

Because we really wanted the house, we agreed to use our savings for the down payment, thinking we could sell our current house quickly and replenish the loss. However, even after coming up with the loan company's initial demands, they would call and say they needed more. We really were not experienced at "haggling" and just kept giving them more money.

We finally reached the point that there was no more to give them, but they wanted $2,000 more for closing costs! My feathers dropped. We both were so disappointed, we almost gave up. We had to give them an answer soon.

I began praying hard that God would help us get the house. To have our hopes so high and get so close, only to have our dream whisked away like a Texas dust twister was devastating. He had promised, "If we asked anything in Christ's name, believing, He would give it" (Matthew 21:22). I really believed God had the answer, and He did.

Frustrated about getting the loan approved, my mind was not on my daily routine. I was searching for a package of pens I thought was in our secretary. I pulled open the bottom drawer and lifted a stack of papers to see if the pens had fallen underneath. What I saw made my stomach jump with excitement.

Jeff had been with the aircraft company for twenty-two years. Because the company was dependent on government funding for much of their orders, they encouraged their employees to purchase government bonds. Jeff had done it for years. The bonds came in the mail, and I had stuck them in the secretary and never cashed them. It took about six months before they matured to purchase price anyway.

To my surprise, I found a stack of bonds that had been there for years. I counted them and added up the totals. We had exactly $2,042 worth of redeemable bonds! God came through again with what some people would call *another* coincidence! However, a true believer's life is FULL of coincidences!

We finally qualified for the loan and moved into our new house in October, 1986. It began another phase of our life together, one that would be full of both blessings and tears.

Chapter 32: Closing the Shop

We were both working hard. Jeff was employed seven days a week and I was running a business that was healthy. Our bills were being paid, but the day came when I no longer wanted to be so busy.

My life was good, but I had much less time to spend "one on one" with the Lord. I missed His fellowship and even though I talked (in my head) all day with Him, I still needed time to spend alone in prayer without interruptions and the nagging fatigue that accompanies hours filled with a demanding career. I began praying God would reveal exactly what He wanted me to do.

Little by little, He caused a sensation of restlessness in my spirit. I now recognize that sensation as a spiritual wind that blows just prior to changes in my lifestyle. He would give me direction when the time was right.

I continued to pray and felt more and more that He wanted me to close the store. I had no idea what I would do with my time if I quit sewing.

I didn't know what God wanted me to do, but I should have known He already had that plan in order.

I investigated the possibility of using my skills in the garment industry. I bought a Dallas paper and called about a job as "first pattern cutter" for Prophecy dress line. They made business suits for career women.

The receptionist answered the phone and transferred me to the personnel department. After giving my experience credentials, I was asked to come in for an interview. The following Thursday, I went to a job interview.

The lady who interviewed me was congenial. I immediately felt comfortable. We talked as she looked through the portfolio of my creations. She was impressed by my skills and asked if I had any questions about the position.

Slightly embarrassed, I asked, "Exactly what is a "first pattern cutter"?"

She chuckled quietly and said. "A first pattern cutter works with a live model, usually a size 10, and makes a pattern of our design. Then, it is revised many times until we decide to keep the design in our line. Whether or not we keep it depends on the complications of the design and cost effectiveness. Should you take the position, you would be the one to do this job. After seeing your work and hearing your experience, I think you are quite capable of doing the job, but I am concerned that you might be terribly bored with our lines. You have created such beautiful formalwear. I'd like to set up an interview for you with another company that is always looking for good designers. Are you familiar with the Victor Costa Company?"

My heart skipped a beat. Of course, I knew about Victor Costa! He had begun his career in Houston making dresses for friends there. He studied at Pratt in Brooklyn, New York, and later spent a year in Paris during the time when Christian Dior was at his peak. He was highly influenced by Dior's sense of dressing women with the classic look of the fifties formality.

By 1975, Costa opened his own boutique in Dallas. He was known as the "King of the Copycats." This was not a disparaging title, as most American designers copied the Paris designers from the beginning of the American garment industry, but Victor Costa was *very good* at it.

In fact, he admitted (and perhaps justified his copying) when he said, "The mirroring of the highest standard has been the basis of our society from Day One. There's a Rolls Royce, a Tiffany, Beluga caviar... and there's a customer who knows and wants what is considered the ultimate. It takes talent to look at the world and see what is in the wind for his customer so she always looks pretty and feels provoked to buy." (*Baltimore Jewish Times,* 1989)

I could hardly believe it when the lady at Prophecy said, "Would you like me to call Victor and set up an interview with him?"

I managed to calmly say, "Of course...I would appreciate that very much," as if I got offers like that every day!

I arrived at Victor Costa, Inc. with my portfolio in hand (several photo albums of my finished products). I met with Carlos, Victor's partner.

He thumbed through my photos and said, "This is very impressive, Ann. Tell me about yourself. Where did you study?"

In my Texas-country-hick-drawl, I told him my background. I hadn't "studied" anywhere. I graduated with a high school degree. I had art lessons, learned to paint, learned to sew, and by this time had about sixteen years of self-taught design school (*God and the "School of Hard Knocks" had been my education*).

He then asked, "Do you work from soft patterns or hard patterns?"

Oh, dear! I had *no* idea what he was talking about! I figured the truth was the best policy, so I said. "I'm sorry, Carlos. I'm not familiar with design terminology. If you'll explain the difference, I'll give you an answer."

He smiled and said, "Soft patterns are shaped on a customer." They are made of muslin. In fact we have a soft pattern in the workshop now for Mrs. Bush, the President's wife. We do a soft pattern for each customer, bring it to the workshop, and place it on a dress form. It is stuffed with polyester batting to form the perfect shape of the customer. Then, we make the garment. When we deliver the dress there are few adjustments beyond that point…and nothing that cannot be done on site. A hard pattern is made of lightweight cardboard copied from the soft pattern. It is used for cutting multiples should the design be accepted into our line."

That's exactly what I'd been doing all along! I was making soft AND hard patterns!

"Oh, I understand." I said. "Then the answer to your question is…I make both types of patterns."

He seemed pleased with my answer and then took me on a tour through the workshop.

There were four designers working at "state-of-the-art" drafting tables.

When we walked into the room, they all fell on top of their designs to hide them. I thought that was strange. We continued on the tour and came back to the office.

"Ann, I think Victor would be very pleased to have you as part of the team. However, there is one test we give our potential designers. They must copy a dress for Victor and bring the finished product back to us. Victor is buying a dress in Houston today and won't be back until tomorrow with a dress he wishes to have in his line. Can you come back tomorrow to meet Victor and get the dress to copy for us? Oh, yes, one other thing. Should you be hired to work here, you must understand none of the other designers will answer any question should you need help. You will have to depend on Victor or me to give you help should it be necessary, that is, if we are here. This is a very competitive field. Do you understand?"

I shook my head "yes" then told him, "I'm in the process of selling my store and finishing my current orders. Would it be a problem to wait for a month to get the copy? I'd rather concentrate fully, rather than be distracted by other obligations."

"Of course, Take your time and call us when you are ready. We'll have something for you then. It is very difficult to find good designers with experience such as yours. I think Victor will agree with my opinion."

I thanked Carlos and left the boutique with my albums. It was all so fantastic I almost floated the rest of the day. It wasn't the pay would be that much better but, in fact, a little less than I was making on my own, but the *prestige* of saying "I'm a designer with Victor Costa" was a heady experience. I would have to pray about this one.

The only negative to the interview was our trip through the workroom. It bothered me that I would work with people that considered me a "threat" all the time. Work relations might not be pleasant and *that* concerned me. A month later I had my direction from the Lord.

After praying about the job offer at Victor Costa, I felt certain I was to stay home during Nisha's high school years. She was a beautiful young lady, very popular with her classmates and, potentially, could have made some really harmful decisions during her teen years, the kinds of decisions that could change a life course. Her development was more important to me than the recognition I might have in my career. I was a mom first...a designer second.

It wasn't an easy decision. I was tempted to grab the one opportunity that might have produced "fame and fortune." The pull was strong to "make a name for myself." Who wouldn't be tempted by that?

One argument Satan threw in my lap was to "evangelize" an area of our culture that evidenced a strong, ungodly appearance. Wouldn't God *want* me to be an influence there? Satan's effort to confuse me was relentless, but because I knew that confusion was one of Satan's tactics, I chose to stay home. I could finally recognize Satan's voice in my head and wanted to give him a "punch in the face."

(1 Corinthians 14:33a "God is *not* the author of confusion" and James 3:16 "Confusion and evil lurk within envy and strife").

I phoned Victor Costa, Inc. and declined the offer they had made. Carlos thanked me for calling and assured me I would be reconsidered anytime I ever needed a job.

Much later, I discovered some facts about Victor Costa, Inc. Even at the time I was making my choice, God knew the future of Victor Costa, Inc.

It seems, due to employee embezzlement and a lawsuit by one of his partners, Victor closed the design shop in 1995. Had I taken the job, my career with him would have been short lived.

Chapter 33: Changes Come

By faith, I opened the store and by faith, I closed it. When the doors of "The Fairy Godmother" locked for the final time, I took the rest of my equipment home to a workshop out back of our house.

Jeff portioned a part of his workshop/barn he built behind our house for a sewing area, separate from the rest of the shop. He didn't want dresses hanging from every door facing and straight pins piercing his feet when he climbed out of bed in the mornings. We joked about him being the only guy on the block that had to put his boots on to go to the bathroom in the middle of the night!

My work area was no larger than it had been at the store, but it was totally private. The phone didn't ring constantly, customers didn't continually interrupt production, and I had plenty of time to visit with God. It was a quiet place and I loved it.

I finally had time to make drapes for the house, decorative pillows for my beds, and placemats and napkins for my formal dining room.

I loved being home for awhile. I could still produce formalwear and yet have the convenience of cooking a pot of beans or doing the laundry at the same time.

Chapter 34: The Bible Study

It was a joy to share our home with all our friends in and out our doors. Eventually, God led us to use our home for a Bible study once a week. A mix of ages and different denominations came. We shared a meal together and discussed the Bible afterwards. Open discussion was lively and beneficial. It was during this time the Lord gave me many illustrations (parables and analogies) that I still use today. The following are some I'll share. Perhaps it will answer some of your questions about the Bible, too.

....

QUESTION: "I know what the scripture says about salvation and I understand that. But what does God do with all those thousands in the world that have *never* heard about Christ or the way to be saved? Will they go to Hell?

ANSWER: Romans 1:19-20 answers that question when Paul spoke of the same issue. "Man *knows* about sin inertly because God reveals it to him.

He can understand his own need for God by looking into the night sky, or seeing a majestic mountain, or viewing anything in nature. It is from those created things that we realize God's eternal power and existence. So nobody has an excuse that they never "heard" about God. He is all around us.

When we "know" God in that way and still choose not to give Him the respect and gratitude He deserves, we become prideful and create our own ideas about who God is and become "blind" to the truth. We think we are so wise, but instead we are fools."

....

QUESTION: "Why do we sometimes not get what we ask for when we pray? Didn't Jesus tell us in Matthew 21:22, "You can ask for *anything* in prayer and, if you *believe* God will give it to you, He will."

ANSWER: James 4: 1-3 put a new twist on that promise and explained why we sometimes do NOT get what we pray for. (My paraphrase)

"Where do fights and wars come from? They come because you want things God doesn't think you should have. You are not satisfied that God says "no" to your desires. You want things so much you would be willing to kill for it. You dream about it, yet you can't seem to obtain it. You don't have it, because you never ask God for it, and when you DO ask, you don't get it because you ask for the wrong reasons. You want that inordinate desire satisfied, if only temporarily, until the next desire comes."

The Lord gave me the following story to illustrate His answer to that question.

A very rich man had two sons. One was an obedient son, always desiring to please his father. The other son was obedient now and then, whenever he wanted something. He knew how to manipulate his father long enough to get what he wanted, but after his desire was satisfied, returned to doing whatever he pleased, regardless of his father's wishes.

Both sons were old enough to drive and came to their father asking for a car. The obedient son came first.

"Hi, Dad, can I ask you something?"

"Sure, son, ask anything you want. I'm all ears."

"Can I have a car of my own? I promise I'll be very careful with it. I'll wash it at least once a week, make sure the oil is changed regularly, and keep all the trash out of it. It doesn't have to be new. Whatever you'd like to provide will be fine. Anytime you want me to run errands for you I'll do it. I could help you get a lot more done that way. If you wanted to use my car I would never object. I'd also be careful who I allowed in the car. I wouldn't want anything to distract me from driving carefully. I know what you expect of me."

Then the other son came asking for a car.

"Hi-ya,Dad! I heard my brother asked you for a car. I thought I'd hit you up for one, too. What do you think? Can I have a car, also?"

He continued, "Let me tell you what I really want. I'd like to have a very classy car. I want a red car, maybe a Corvette with a 505 engine, 18 inch wheels that are 9 inches deep, full window tint, leather interior, on board navigation system with a DVD entertainment package that would really impress the girls, you know what I mean?"

Catching his breath he said, "I know you are really "picky" about the cars around here being clean and all. If I forget, I know you'd remind me. My friends and I would have a lot of fun cruising around picking up girls. It could really put me in a better position to be part of the "in crowd," the ones that set the pace around here?"

The father raised an eyebrow and asked, "Will you share that car with me if I ask?"

"Well, Dad, that's a lot to ask. If I can get that car, I'm going to be using it all the time. I've got to be seen as the *real* owner of the car to get all the attention it will bring. I suppose if you didn't keep it very long, and I wasn't using it for awhile, I'd let you use it. But don't ask me to run errands for you. I intend to LIVE in that car! Man! I can't wait to get my hands on it!"

Now...which of the sons do you think got what he wanted?

....

QUESTION: Can you ever be too busy doing good things?

ANSWER: The Lord gave me a precious illustration one summer morning, while mulling over many jobs I had to do before the Sunday lesson. I loved the freedom I had in my job, but there were so many interruptions, each day passed with little time for myself. I was telling God how tired I was, and then I asked Him, "How am I going to keep up this pace, Lord? I know I am doing what you asked me to do, but my strength is waning."

He said. "Ann, look at that oak tree in front of the porch."

I did but all I saw was a tree. Then I looked closer. There was a small sparrow perched on a lower limb. His head twisted from side to side. He fluttered his wings and then began an ascent upward, hopping from one limb to the next until he finally took flight from the top of the tree.

Gently God spoke. "Remember how I told you I am the vine and you are the branches? (John15:5) "I am the vine and you are the branches. Whoever stays close to me and I stay close to them will produce a lot of fruit, for without me, you can do nothing."

"Yes, Lord. I remember."

"Well, my branches are there for people to "rest" upon, but they are *not* supposed to be a permanent resting place. Instead, you have felt that the "little ones" I gave you would perish if you were not there to "hold them up."

Look around you. I have *lots* of branches on my tree. They are all capable of holding the weight that comes to them, but if you hold on to the "creatures" that come to you and do not let them go, they will never take flight to the destination I have planned for them."

His point was well taken. I vowed to let go of my "little ones" into His care.

He was perfectly capable of bringing other "branches" into their lives to give them rest.

....

QUESTION: What does a parent say to a child who wants to be accepted by those you do not think are best for them?

ANSWER: This incident gave the answer. One afternoon, our daughter told me she had been invited to a big party. She was a freshman, and longed to be accepted by the "in" crowd. She said she wanted to go to be a Christian "witness" to all the kids there, because she would not be drinking, even if liquor was present.

She reasoned, "Even Jesus went to parties 'cause it says in the Bible that people called Him a wine-bibber and a party-animal"(Luke 7:33-34). "John the Baptist came fasting, and you said he had a devil. I come eating and drinking and you call me a glutton and wine-bibber, a friend of tax collectors and sinners!"

The draw to be accepted at that age is incredibly strong. Nisha was tempted to join the crowd that "rode the fence." They went to church on Sunday after a night of partying wildly.

We can all remember times we made poor choices based on our desire to be accepted.

(This illustration came instantly to my mind) I asked her "If you were an ice cube placed in a hot glass of tea what would happen to you?"

"I'd melt." she replied.

"Exactly," I said, "but suppose you and several more ice cubes were placed in the hot tea. What would happen then?"

"I guess we'd all melt eventually, but we would have cooled the tea some."

"I agree. Your Christian witness works like that, too. You can associate with people who have no interest in being obedient to God and soon you won't care about being obedient either. You'll become just like them.

However, if you were to jump into that hot tea and then quickly jump back into the freezer again, you would maintain your power to change the tea, right? Little by little you could have an effect without losing yourself.

Honey, the power of Satan to draw us into sin is great. It doesn't take much persuasion to get us to forsake right living. He often draws us away from a good relationship with God by using innocent desires that grow from a thought to an action that harm our fellowship with God.

Eventually, we do things we never thought we'd ever do. At the same time we justify our actions. Satan wants us to believe that "right is wrong and "wrong is right."

So, either soak yourself in the Word of God and prayer to stay strong or get with other believers that are spiritually stronger than you. THEN you can be an effective witness with power."

We all have wrong desires in our hearts, and Satan knows the weak areas of desire we each harbor. Given the right set of circumstances, we all could fail in our walk with Christ.

(James 1:13-15..."Don't use the excuse that God knows your weakness and tempts you with it. God cannot be tempted to do wrong and He certainly doesn't tempt you to do wrong. When you are tempted to do wrong it is because *you want* to do wrong. Then your desire swells into action. You disagree with God about what He says is the right thing to do. So you choose to do the opposite. This choice separates us from a good relationship with God. It is death to our spiritual nature.")

....

QUESTION: What will Heaven be like?

ANSWER: (God can reveal it to you)

Prayer became a wonderful habit of mine, but before I made it habitual, I had used prayer as more of a "hot line" to God when things got harried. However, with the Bible study and soaking myself once more in the scriptures I found that prayer became a more increasing need.

Every morning after Jeff left for work, before the sun came up, I'd grab another cup of coffee and saunter out to our patio to talk with God. It was there, laid back in the chaise lounge, I had a wonderful "vision."

Now, it wasn't like the vision I had of Satan years before, where the door blew open and all that, but rather a quiet understanding that dawned in my spirit and embellished itself in the night sky.

I was praying by thanking God for all He was and all He had done for me over the years, just praising Him while I looked into the star-studded sky. I realized my own insignificance. Then, suddenly, I saw (in my "mind's eye") a glimpse of Heaven   It must have been galaxies away and seemed suspended high above for only a short time.

I saw a huge crowd of people (millions) surrounding a very bright light. It shone miles into the heavens, much like those beacons new businesses rent to advertise their grand openings, only *much* brighter. The light seemed to go in all directions and fade away miles from its source. The whole sensation was more of a revelation than an actual sighting. That's hard to explain, but I can still remember it clearly.

I lay there with a severe longing to be in that crowd that was singing and crowding around that great light. I knew instinctively that the source of the light was God, himself. For a moment's time, I was allowed to "see" the majesty of God as it will be in heaven. I still get "homesick" to be there when I remember it. What a wonderful revelation!

(Acts 2:17) "And it shall come to pass in the last days," says God," I will pour out of my Spirit upon all flesh: and your sons and your daughters shall prophesy, and your young men shall see visions, and your old men shall dream dreams."

Chapter 35: Manic/Depressive

Close friendships grew from that home study that last even today. The lessons from God's Word sank deeply into our beings and made a difference in the way we lived. Our lives were changed by the way God convinced us to trust His scriptures and believe them.

Gradually, each of us took that knowledge and formed lives that would have been totally different had we not experienced that study. We were changed, and incredibly blessed.

Four years later, like a soft wind blowing in a different direction, the study disbanded as each of us went other places.

Some moved away with job changes. Some married and joined their spouses in other towns. As I told you previously, Kitty died at age fifty-seven, diagnosed with advanced diabetes, she succumbed to a heart attack.

Jeff's career with airplane manufacturing had been successful. He had climbed up the corporate "ladder" one rung at a time. At first, he wore a T-shirt and jeans and was a metal former, hammering out airplane parts. At the end of his career, he wore nice slacks and neckties and was planning meetings or going on corporate trips. He had taken what God had given him and been fruitful. The "ride" had been furious, but God's grace had been sufficient. I'm sure God smiled.

My life had been very blessed also. God had re-channeled my manic state into prolific productivity (which is a *good* thing!) For example, in one year of my career, I made 156 formal gowns. That's an average of over 1/2 dress per day, many of which were wedding gowns! Of course, it took longer to make a wedding gown than a bridesmaid dress, so often I completed *more* than one half of a dress per day! (It all worked out as most ladies wanted to wear more than one half of her dress and many times my deadlines were for the same day.) I had some really good employees working for me who did all the cutting, hand finish, pressing, keeping the store clean and helping sell products. The Lord had certainly taught me how to focus my mind instead of "bouncing off the walls," getting nothing done.

He had changed my depressive state into trust in Him when things went wrong. Instead of dwelling on the negative, I learned to think on the good things in my life (Philippians 4:6-8), "Don't worry about anything. Instead, pray about everything asking God for help. By doing so, God's peace will fill your heart and MIND through Christ. You won't even know how He does it. It just happens. And last, but not least…discipline your mind to think on true things, honest things, right things, pure things, lovely things, positive things. If there is *anything* good in your life, think about *those* things."

Chapter 36: Autoharp Champion

Jeff and I loved music and had sung together since high school choir. So in our spare time while we were still working, we learned to play musical instruments. He played guitar and I played the autoharp, a folk instrument that Maybelle Carter made famous. On weekends that I wasn't scheduled for a wedding job, we took off to remote areas in our RV to make music with others at music festivals. It was a wonderful release from the job stress we both had. We enjoyed our weekend travel so much we planned for the day we could do it full time. That dream came true when we retired, sold our house, and went from 2,700 square feet of living space to less than 400! We traveled all over the USA full-time for nine years.

By God's grace in 2002, I won the International Autoharp Championship at the Walnut Valley Bluegrass Festival, Winfield Kansas. I only mention this for those of you who feel that a diagnosis of "severe paranoid schizophrenia" will keep you bound to an inferior life of being medicated the rest of your life just to function in a normal way. I am proof this is not true.

There was only one time in my incredible journey from insanity to a normal life that made me worry. I began what seemed to be a relapse of schizophrenia after we retired.

Chapter 37: Insane again?

We didn't get to travel immediately after we retired. At the same time we were selling our house and moving to our small farm in east Texas, Jeff's mother, who was 89 years old, became very sick and needed full-time care. She did not want to live in a nursing home, so Jeff's niece, who lived near our farm, took her in. We volunteered to sit with her daily while Jeff's niece worked. We drove about 70 miles a day (round trip) to do so. It was a circumstance I hadn't expected. Our hopes for travel were put "on hold."

Along with this change in our plans, our daughter and her husband found jobs in a town near us, sold their house, bought an RV and moved to the farm with us. We shared the same concrete pad and canopy. It was a move I hadn't expected.

I could not change my circumstances, and praying about it did not seem to help. I began obsessing about the negatives.

Once more, I became paranoid. My fears took over my mind, and I went into a deep depression. I withdrew from my family, thinking they were conspiring against me. My daughter was so concerned, she insisted I go with her to a health food store and buy some hormone replacement cream, thinking it would help change my mood swings. I cried often, and though I continued praying God would relieve me of my misery, I saw no results.

Finally, one day as I was frantically digging in the garden to get my mind off negatives, Jeff came near and I asked him to get another digging tool from the barn for me. I don't remember exactly how he answered, but whatever he said threw me into a raging fit! I cursed and screamed until finally, I realized I must be going through an "episode."

The next day, I made an appointment with a nearby psychiatrist. I knew I had to have some help!

Chapter 38: Course Correction

I entered the medical office, knowing I must rely on a professional to help me. My exercise, diet and meditation were not working anymore. I had lost control of what had balanced me for years. Questions flooded my mind. Why had God not answered my prayers? Why had He seemingly stopped "talking" to me? What had I done wrong?

Then the receptionist said, "The doctor will see you now, Mrs. Norris."

Dr. _____ had a calm demeanor as he leaned back in his chair at a large table that could have accommodated a corporate meeting. I suppose that was to give the psychological impression that I was just as important as he was?

Then, he asked, "Now why have you come to see me today, Mrs. Norris?"

I got right to the point. I told him my past experience with insanity. I told him how I'd managed to keep balanced with exercise, diet, and prayer. I said I'd not been on any kind of medication and learned to function well without it, but I'd lost control and felt I was losing my mind again. I waited despondently to hear I needed to be facilitated again to regain control.

To my surprise, he chuckled and said, "Mrs. Norris I think you have honed your "coping skills" well. I don't think you are losing control of your mind. I suspect you are having some hormonal issues. How long has it been since you've seen your gynecologist?"

I recalled and told him, "Probably five years or more. I really can't remember exactly. Since I had a hysterectomy years ago and no problematic symptoms thereafter, I didn't feel an annual exam was so important."

"Well," he said, "go see your gynecologist and get a thorough exam. If he doesn't find some abnormality, then come back and see me again and I'll help you get through this." With that he stood, shook my hand, and took my money.

I followed his advice and made an appointment.

Chapter 39: Ovarian Cancer?

I sat in the waiting room at the OB-GYN clinic and filled out all the necessary paperwork, then met Dr. Trist, after I sat in a hospital gown atop an examining table for what seemed like a long time. He looked over my chart and said he would be able to tell me more after my exam.

I've *never* enjoyed a pelvic exam (what woman does?!) but the more he probed, the more concern I saw on his face. He said, "I think I want to do a sonogram, Mrs. Norris. If you'll step into the room across the hall, my X-ray tech will prepare you for this.

"Hmmm"...I thought ...*I've never done that before in a check-up??"*

When we met in his office after the sonogram, the doctor told me I had a large tumor attached to one of my ovaries. He wanted me to go to the hospital X-ray lab and get a full sonogram first thing Monday morning. He said to bring my overnight bag, in case the results were what he expected. He would do emergency surgery that day. With a somber note, he added, "Ovarian cancer, Mrs. Norris, is nothing to play around with. It's aggressive and ugly. But let's not jump to conclusions till we see the size of the growth."

With that, I left and numbly walked out to the car where Jeff was waiting for me.

"The doctor said I had a growth attached to my ovary. He wants me to get a full sonogram at the hospital Monday morning."

We both were concerned, but not worried. I prayed that all would be well and, if not, my God would get me through this, too. After all, He'd proven Himself time and time again in my life.

Monday's sonogram proved that indeed I had a growth the size of a small grapefruit clinging to my left ovary. Surgery was scheduled, and I was prepped and ready.
Thankfully, Dr. Trist's wife was a pathologist and agreed to be in surgery with him, so we could get

immediate results of testing the growth for malignancy.

When I was in recovery, he came in beaming from ear to ear. The tumor was benign, but the results proved to me that God's healing of my mind was sufficient. I didn't have to fear insanity again!

Chapter 40: Total Peace

Now, I live in a peaceful place with beautiful meadows surrounding. The morning sounds are calming. Birds chirp while gentle breezes blow, tinkling the wind chimes that hang in the trees nearby. I awake to the smell of fresh mown grass. I am incredibly blessed.

As I look back on my journey to sanity, I have nothing to say, but God is good. It was by His guidance and patience I found emotional and mental stability. I simply followed Biblical principles and learned to trust my heavenly Father more through the years.

Like Paul said in Ephesians 2: 8-10 "I was made whole by my belief, and even my belief came as a gift from God. I was not made whole by my actions. Or else I would have become proud. My sanity was created through Jesus for His good works. God's way was declared so that I could BE that way." *Totally SANE!*

To my readers:

I never would have written this story if I hadn't heard the "voice" of my God encouraging me to do so.

To reveal all the ugliness in my life is not an easy task, but it has been a cleansing, much like the little "man" in my attic dream said it would be. He would not clean that attic, but He would tell me how to do it.

If you feel life has treated you unfairly,

If you have lost all hope and wallow in despair,

If you have fears that bind you from becoming all you have potential to be,

If you have no purpose in life,

Then I pray my book has encouraged you to find the same Light I found.

"Trust in the Lord with all your heart; and don't be partial to your own understanding. In all your ways acknowledge Him, and He shall direct your paths" (Proverbs 3:5-6)

Follow the voice of the great "I Am." He is waiting for you.

"And you shall seek Me and find Me when you search for Me with all your heart"(Jeremiah 29:13).

....

"Father, I pray this reader will let go of their pride, their fears and the many reasons the *other voice* gives them to doubt you. In Jesus' name, I pray that you will enfold them in your love and acceptance as you did for me, so that they, too, may know the joy and peace you can bring to their life. Amen."

Acknowledgments

I've had many friends through life who have encouraged me to write my story. They would say, "You've got to write a book!" or "Let me know when your book is ready. I want one!" Without their words pushing me, I probably would never have written my story.

A few years ago I was invited to attend the Whyte Dove writer's group in my area. It was here I first exposed my *whole* story to those in the group. They were gentle with their criticisms and continued to strengthen my confidence as I dredged my memories and sifted through them, albeit painful at times. I also thank Terrell AronSpeer, one of this group, for helping me post my book on Kindle and then on Create Space. Had he not been determined this writing was going to be published, the book would have remained on nothing but a memory stick because I don't know much more about a computer than the use of the "on / off" button.

I also owe a great debt of gratitude to my friend and editor, Cindy Holbrook, who with her expertise, loaded my book with an extra 3 pages of commas I'd left out, along with suggestions for making some of my statements clearer. She, indeed, performed a labor of love and I will ever be indebted to her.

My sister, Jean, gave me the best advice of anyone when she said "Ann, you need to eliminate all information except what pertains to your sickness and healing." So my book became 1,500 words thinner. (Aren't you glad?)

However, the greatest influence on my writing has been the "voice" of my God who spoke this book into being when He rescued me from myself. He deserves all the credit. It was He who told me to write it all. So truly, it is a sacrifice of humility given to Him. May He have all the accolades, if there are any.

Margaret Jackson

About the Author

Ann Norris has been a "Jack of all trades and master of a few."
- Housewife and mother (non-paying)
- Professional Artist and teacher
- Professional Furniture Refinisher
- Professional Seamstress and Designer
- Wedding Store Owner / Operator
- Full-time RV traveler for 9 years
- International Autoharp Champion, 2002
- Professional Autoharp Instructor
- Professional Vocal and Instrumental Entertainer
- (and if you buy this book)…A Professional Author

She resides in Texas with her husband, Jeff, on a hay and pecan farm with their 4 cats and 3 dogs. They celebrated their 50th year of marriage this year.